CECIL HAYES
ART OF DECORATIVE DETAILS

CECIL HAYES

ART OF

DECORATIVE

CREATIVE WAYS TO

DESIGN THE HOME

DETAILS

OF YOUR DREAMS

WATSON-GUPTILL PUBLICATIONS
NEW YORK

In this client's home, I created a simple buffet unit, which combined framed moldings with flat-panel side units. The center component of the buffet is 8 inches deeper than the two side units, and the depth separating the center and sides allow the doors on the center section to carry a different detail. Three different sized moldings were applied on the doors, which made the unit the center of attention.

Editorial Director: Victoria Craven
Editor: Martha Moran
Contributing Editor: Tara Blackwell
Designer: Julie Duquet
Production Manger: Alyn Evans

First published in the United States by
Watson-Guptill Publications
Nielsen Business Media,
a division of the Nielsen Company
770 Broadway
New York, New York 10003
www.watsonguptill.com

Printed in China

First printing, 2007
1 2 3 4 5 6 7 8 9 / 15 14 13 12 11 10 09 08 07

ISBN-13: 978-0-8230-9974-0
ISBN-10: 0-8230-9974-1

CONTENTS

Introduction: It's All in the Decorative Details   9

Overview   12

1 ⊲ A DECORATIVE DETAILING PRIMER   15

2 ⊲ FLOORING DETAILS   27

3 ⊲ WALL AND TRIM DETAILS   39

4 ⊲ WINDOW AND WINDOW TREATMENT DETAILS   75

5 ⊲ ARCHITECTURAL DETAILS   91

6 ⊲ FURNITURE DETAILS   117

7 ⊲ FABRIC AND SOFT COVERING DETAILS   137

8 ⊲ TRANSFORMATION IMAGINATION   151

Working Drawings for Cecil's Original Furniture Designs   172

Photo Credits   173

Resources   174

Index   176

In one home, I used molding to play up an unusual picture window with a view into the client's walled garden. Instead of installing a typical drapery treatment, I framed the window in simple carved molding. The arched transom was also framed out with molding, and decorative corbels were added directly beneath the horizontal framing member. A rich pecan stain contrasts with the cream-colored walls to draw your attention out into the garden.

I dedicate this book to my niece, Shea Burrows Orgill. Thank you for eighteen years of being a forceful presence at Cecil's Designers Unlimited. Your management of the office allowed me to do what I do best: be an artist.

Special dedication to my husband, Arzell Powell. After twenty-three years of working together, I am so happy that we still leave the office together.

And, of course, much love to Mikal (Teandre) and Mikala.

ACKNOWLEDGMENTS

As in all things, it takes a large circle of connected minds to transform thoughts into tangible results. *Cecil Hayes Art of Decorative Details* came from a concept of teaching and viewing that I always believed was worthy of presentation in the form of a book. While the initial thought may have been mine, without the following individuals this book would not have been possible. I acknowledge you and Thank You with all of my heart.

My clients: Thank you for allowing me to create the beautiful interiors that grace these pages.

The vendors who have graciously allowed me to feature their products and installations within these pages: Ann Sacks, Butterick, Lowitz & Company, M&J Trimming, Mark Wilkinson Furniture, Nightshades (Christine Kilger), Ravan Incorporated, Walker-Zanger, and Waverly. Thank you for the wonderful images you have shared with me.

Special thanks to Tim Ribar, my primary photographer on this book, who went above and beyond the call of duty and did whatever was necessary to get me the best quality photos in the shortest time possible so I could meet all my deadlines.

Finally, I didn't forget you, Tara Blackwell. Thanks so much for always being there for me. You have a very special gift. You can always understand my writing and spelling and know how to make the necessary corrections without altering my concepts. What a gal!

INTRODUCTION

It's All in the Decorative Details

WHAT MAKES THE most powerful statement in interior design? What adds life and depth to a design concept? What can take an interior from "drab" to "fab" with just a little effort? The answer, in my opinion, is all in the decorative details—they are the heart of my personal design style.

For years, I was proud to proclaim that I didn't have a signature design style, and that I designed for clients within *their* chosen style, not my signature look. About five years ago, however, I was taken aback when one of my clients disputed this. He said that although he couldn't put his finger on exactly what my style was, I *did* have one. "It makes you feel good," he said. "It's in the mix of materials and details." As I thought about it, I began to see that he was right.

I am known for my ability to combine pattern and textures into warm and friendly interiors. I've also been praised for using decorative detailing to heighten the effect. I just never thought of that as a signature style. To me, it was always about finding a special detail (or details) to make a space beautiful and to make my clients feel good about their homes.

As a professional interior designer, I have had ample opportunity to perfect my decorative detailing. Personally, I have never worried about whether or not my details would "work"; if I liked the idea, I gave it a try. I'm certainly not saying that I never made mistakes. Once in a while, I've had to change something out or try something else. But, that is how we learn . . . and I'm still learning.

I see this book as a continuation of my previous book, *9 Steps to Beautiful Living: Dream, Design, and Decorate Your Home with Style.* In that book, I took you, the reader, step by step through my personal design process and offered tips and techniques to help you create the interior design of your dreams. I also shared a lot of technical information, including simple formulas designed to guarantee successful results. While you can certainly get a lot from this book without reading *9 Steps*, I recommend you do read it because it lays a solid foundation for everything I will discuss here.

Once you have completed your initial interior design, you're ready to take the next step—adding the decorative details that make your décor dazzle. *Art of Decorative Details* will teach you, in precise detail, how to achieve the finished and polished "wow!" look of a professional interior designer. This book is about kicking your design skills up a notch, about taking your basic interior design and refining it. Think of the basic room designs we created together in *9 Steps* as plain vanilla pound cake. In *Art of Decorative Details*, I give you all the tools you need to dress up that plain cake and create something truly original and spectacular.

My goal is to open your eyes and to make you aware of your surroundings. I want you to look at things differently and to learn that you can find ideas everywhere: flip through magazines; walk through homes; note interesting materials, unusual objects, striking combinations, and fabulous finishes. I want you to be inspired! Keep a small

I found an old stool at the flea market one day that had great bones, but it was in really poor condition. Originally it was old and unloved, and I felt that it needed not only to be refinished, but also reupholstered. I actually had a yard of the fabulous floral print fabric, and I loved the way the daisies danced across it. Almost as if the stool was speaking to me, I suddenly thought that it would also be fun to use the fabric as the inspiration for the refinishing, too. So we painted the stool black and I hired an artist to carry the daisy theme on to the structure. Once finished, the stool was given a clear coat of polyurethane to seal it. When the upholstery was completed, I had a whimsical accent piece that I absolutely adore!

In creating a warm-color accent wall in this room, I added a decorative twist in the form of an unusual wall niche. The niche started as a high side window, which wasn't needed for lighting but was in the perfect location to display art. After hanging a closed blind in it (to keep the exterior view intact), we dry-walled over the existing window. The unusual shape of the niche was designed to highlight the owner's art objects. The niche and the warm red wall color combine to create a dramatic focal point.

notebook handy so you can jot down notes about the things that appeal to you. If you like something, write it down, and you will always have a source to refer to when you need inspiration. For me, great concepts often come from public places: hotel lobbies, restaurants, banks, etc. I recommend looking at ceilings, walls, floors, and even floral arrangements for creative inspiration.

The whole idea behind decorative detailing is to create change in a look by adding to what already exists, to add little touches that bring oomph to your décor. I define *details* as items that would not normally be a part of the generic whole. These are special additions that accomplish one (or more!) of the following:

- ✤ Add pizzazz to the look
- ✤ Conceal a non-removable distraction
- ✤ Create a one-of-a-kind décor
- ✤ Pull the decoration (or decorative scheme) together
- ✤ Solve a problem

To approach detailing properly, you have to believe that it is important, that it makes a beautiful thing better, and, most of all, that it can be achieved.

I suppose that I must have learned my decorative detailing lessons early in life. In fact, I truly can't remember a time when I didn't notice decorative details. I think I learned a lot of these lessons from my mother, who worked two jobs yet still made all of my clothes when I was growing up. She thought nothing of tailoring a purchased pattern, and was a stickler for proper finishing. Everyone complimented her on her sewing technique and marveled that her clothing never looked homemade (and this was back in the day when everybody knew how to sew).

Mom insisted on quality materials. She felt that it was more economical to get the best she could afford, and that philosophy extended down to the trims. No cheap buttons for my mother! She may not have used many buttons, but whenever she did, they were elegant, often understated, and usually exquisitely made, just like her clothing. My mother believed in putting her best efforts into the details.

When I was away at college, my girlfriends always made an event out of the days that I received a package from home. I first always had to model every article of clothing that my mother sent me and then I would pass it around to be admired up close. By the reaction of my friends, you would have thought they were attending a couture fashion extravaganza! On the contrary, I was completely jaded. My mother had been sewing for my entire life, and I just thought it was normal for everyone to have clothing of this caliber. However, when I started letting some of my friends borrow my clothes, I got a firsthand lesson in how appearance (and environment) can enhance self-esteem. It was probably one of the most profound lessons of my life.

In décor, as in couture clothing, it's the small things that make the end result sing. The touches don't have to be expensive, and are often better for being understatedly elegant, but they add immeasurably to the completed whole. Often, decorative details are invented out of necessity: Either something isn't working decoratively or there is another type of problem that is getting in the way. To most people, that would be a catastrophe, but to me, a problem is just another opportunity to be creative. I have found that problems have a way of waking up your creative juices, and once that happens you will never view design problems in the same way again. When I see a design difficulty, rather than wishing it would go away, I face it head-on and direct my thoughts to turning the "problem" into something special. Believe me, over the years these potential troublemakers have contributed to some of my best design details.

So, how do you take a problem and turn it into a positive element? First, start by defining the problem. What is it that isn't working for you? Once you know that, you can start creating a solution. And believe me, solving the problem doesn't always require rethinking the entire project. Often, it's as simple as making a minor change.

There are also those details that conceal things, particularly structural or mechanical things, which happen to be located in the wrong place. You can't remove a support column or a heating duct, but you can de-emphasize them or even transform their appearance.

Details don't have to be permanent additions to a décor, either. In fact, table settings and holiday accents are some of the most widely used examples of temporary detailing. These decorative details may have a short lifespan, but they add festive impact to any occasion.

Details come in all shapes and sizes and, as you will see throughout the book, they are my very good friends. I invite them into all of my decorating installations. In fact, these little gems are one of the hallmarks of my design concepts. In truth, adding art and accessories (including detailing) is my favorite part of the whole design process! And if I can learn to use creative details to add pizzazz to my interior installations, I firmly believe that you can, too. Once you do, you'll wonder how you ever got along without them.

Happy detailing!

Ceil

The story behind this unique wine "cellar" is told on page 111.

OVERVIEW

I truly believe that decorative details are one of the major tenets of unique interior designing. Until you've tried them, you just won't believe the difference they can make in an interior. So, before we begin, here is a quick overview of what I will be covering.

CHAPTER 1 ✤ A Decorative Detailing Primer

What is detailing and why do we even want to be bothered with it? Here I discuss what it means to me (interiors with panache instead of just plain good looks), and share my rules for creating decorative details. I also show how you can apply my philosophy of decorative detailing to your home regardless of when it was originally decorated. This mini "book within a book" is full of creative exercises and projects to help you develop your eye for creative detailing.

CHAPTER 2 ✤ Flooring Details

Despite the fact that flooring is always underfoot, it tends to be overlooked by many people when it comes to decorative detailing. This can be due to many reasons, but frequently it is because flooring often comes preinstalled in so many purchased homes. Floor details can be created with stone, ceramic inlays, wood, metal, rugs, carpet, glass tiles, even leather. In a preexisting floor, decorative detailing can also be created with paint or stain.

CHAPTER 3 ✤ Wall and Trim Details

Walls are a fabulous place to add decorative detailing and offer nearly infinite possibilities, such as molding, wallpaper, paint, metal, mirrors, glass, tile (including stone), wood, and fabric, to name just a few. Here, I will walk you through some of my installations and show you how each of these elements can furnish the definitive decorative detailing.

CHAPTER 4 ✤ Window and Trim Details

Window coverings of soft materials (such as drapery, cornices, valances, and fabric shades) are readily familiar to most homeowners. Shoji screens and decorative treatments based on the use of wood and wood moldings, however, may be something entirely new. Then there are window treatments based upon decorative elements such as finials, tassels, etc., that you might not necessarily even think of as window coverings (because what do they cover anyway?). There's no denying that successful window treatments—whether opulent or understated—must work as part of the wall décor. I'll show you why window details are one area where thinking outside of the box can have a big payoff!

CHAPTER 5 ✣ Architectural Details

Architectural details make use of the architectural elements of a space, whether structural or nonstructural. (For the record, structural elements cannot be removed without compromising the structural integrity of the space. Nonstructural elements, on the other hand, have been added purely for aesthetics.) Over the course of my career I've seen many homes where the architectural elements begged for enhancement: fireplaces that wanted to do more than breathe fire, staircases that wanted to do more than extend from one floor to the next, and soffits that wanted not only to drop from the ceiling but to be drop-dead gorgeous at the same time. All of these things are possible with the application of the proper decorative detail, and this chapter shows you how.

CHAPTER 6 ✣ Furniture Details

Creating custom-detailed furniture has always been one of my passions, and the concepts and designs I present in this chapter were professionally designed by me for you. It would be a major undertaking for you to create your own custom furniture and/or special detailing completely from scratch, because so much specialized knowledge is required. (You really need to know about scale, construction methods, available materials, and finishing techniques to successfully design a piece of furniture.) I'll show you how to modify furniture details to suit your preferences—especially if you work hand-in-glove with a cabinetmaker. All of the furniture featured in this chapter started out on paper as working drawings, which contain exact measurements, specifications for components, and diagrams for assembly. I've included six of these working drawings beginning on page 172. Feel free to take them to your cabinetmaker for reproduction/modification to suit your needs!

CHAPTER 7 ✣ Fabric and Soft Covering Details

Fabric is such an essential element in our lives that many of us tend to forget about it in the search for the perfect creative detail. In reality, this material has many usages—from upholstery, to wall treatments, to drapery, to throw pillows, and beyond. Fabric and soft trims are one of the biggest spurs to decorative detailing that I can imagine. Fabric can be sewed, glued, stapled, cut, shaped, and otherwise manipulated. If you're looking for versatility, fabric is the detail element for you. Come along with me and I'll show you new and exciting ways to work with fabric!

CHAPTER 8 ✣ Transformation Imagination

This is probably my favorite chapter because it's all about using decorative details to spark the imagination. The examples featured here run the gamut from found objects that I used as innovative accents, to items that I completely repurposed, to using decorative details to create or enhance theme rooms for both children and adults. This type of design detailing draws heavily upon the imagination, and it's so much fun that I strongly encourage you to give it a try. You'll find the process addictive!

A DECORATIVE DETAILING PRIMER

Most detailing concepts can be applied after the total decoration is complete. In other words, you can live with a room for months—or even years!—yet still come back after the fact and add exciting details.

LIFE ITSELF IS all about details. In order to understand this, you may have to rethink the word *detail*. To me, detail equals imagination, which is a force of unseen energy within you. This energy can only be expressed through the creative process, which involves making an idea tangible. We are all gifted with imagination. We have only to reenergize the power of creativity within us to stimulate our imaginations.

Developing creativity will encourage you to imagine change, not just to improve something, but also to empower your mind. For me, there is no greater joy than when a collection of my creative ideas is assembled into a room, or an object for visual enjoyment. That, to me, is *art*. Art can be one single dot on a canvas or one thousand dots on a canvas. Art has a way of changing the way we look at our surroundings. Art is fun! Art is life!

Decorative detailing is not rocket science. After all, adding trim to a throw pillow will not blow the feathers to kingdom come! Similarly, detailing a wall with paint will only change its color, not its structural integrity. Don't allow yourself to get caught up in the fear of the process. This is art. It's meant to be fun!

So relax. Open yourself up to your sense of fun. Got it? Great! *Now* you're ready to begin creating your own custom look. As you go through these exercises, don't worry about getting things right or wrong. Just give it a try.

Cecil sits amidst a few of the items she uses to create her decorative detail concepts: fabrics, soft trims, wooden moldings, throw pillows, and unusual art pieces.

Mikala's preschool art project explores the concept of creating with shapes.

Here, Mikala's project explores color.

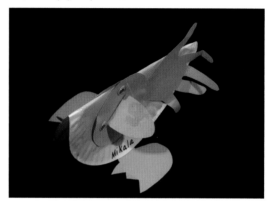

Multiple materials in a combination art project created by Mikala.

My favorite of Mikala's three-dimensional art projects.

BACK TO SCHOOL: THE EARLY YEARS

Young children begin their journey of learning with toys and projects, which develop the imagination. Children's art projects are all about adding details to a plain sheet of paper and, in the process, being creative with simple materials. In my opinion, this is the right approach to learning. At about the age of ten, however, the school curriculum changes and creative thinking becomes secondary to the learning process. By the time we reach adulthood, many of us have forgotten all about being creative. In fact, if it were not for those early childhood art projects, I believe that we would all think only inside the box. Exercises in creative detailing, including art projects, lead to the development of great minds, including doctors and research scientists who must learn to think creatively.

There's absolutely nothing like seeing the world again through the eyes of a child! I am fortunate to have four-year-old Mikala in my life. She is in this early childhood period of creative exploration and her art projects were the inspiration for the lessons in this chapter. These lessons mimic, on a more sophisticated level, Mikala's own journey through creative detailing.

CREATIVE DETAILING: AN ART LESSON IN SIMPLICITY

All things can be accomplished if you understand the process, and the art of detailing is a process involving awareness and imagination. In our artist's imagination, we are not concerned with inventing a material such as paper. Instead, we imagine all the ways we could use and manipulate that paper—by the way we color it, cut it, fold it, etc.

There are three major elements that make up all decorative details: shape, texture/finish, and color. This holds true whether your medium is hard (tile) or soft (pillows).

The following projects are lessons in how to use shape, texture/finish, and/or color as elements in your design details.

SHAPE: THE FIRST DESIGN ELEMENT ✤ Shape alone can be used to create a decorative detail. The design detailing possibilities are as endless as the shapes and combinations of shapes you imagine.

Project 1 ✤ Our first project is a lesson in creative visualization. Consider all the different shapes that can be made out of a square. As you can see, many design detail shapes can be cut from a basic 12-inch x 12-inch square of neutral, beige ceramic tile. Most of these shapes are easy for the average do-it-yourselfer to cut, even when the material is tile. The round and curved shapes, however, are more of a challenge, and although difficult for the home handyman (or ma'am), they are quite simple for a professional tile setter or anyone who is experienced at cutting tile.

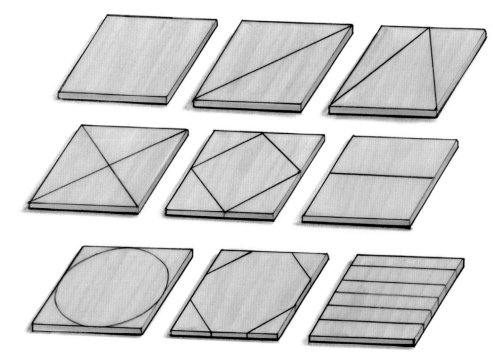

Isn't it amazing the number of shapes that can be cut from a single 12-inch x 12-inch ceramic tile?

Project 2 ✠ Now, let's create a tile detail using the various shapes which can be cut from that 12-inch x 12-inch tile. Here, I've arranged squares, triangles, and octagons to create an interesting backsplash pattern. The good news about creative detailing is that, by simply changing the arrangement of shapes, you can create original, personal designs. In fact, the same shapes can be easily recombined and rearranged into enough patterns to create a different backsplash design detail for you and a hundred friends and family members! The combinations are infinite.

An 18-inch backsplash created from a combination of simple tile shapes.

TEXTURE: THE SECOND DESIGN ELEMENT ✠ Texture can also be used to create beautiful decorative details, and this backsplash project is a good example of how to employ texture as a design detail.

Project 3 ✠ Using the same shapes from Projects 1 and 2, let's see what the introduction of texture does to the monochromatic tile. In addition to the smooth texture of the beige tile, we are going to add a touch of texture. Texture can be added by mixing smooth ceramic tiles with tiles that have relief designs, stone tiles, metal tiles, or glass tiles. Here, the tile pattern is given more depth and a little oomph by the addition of textural details.

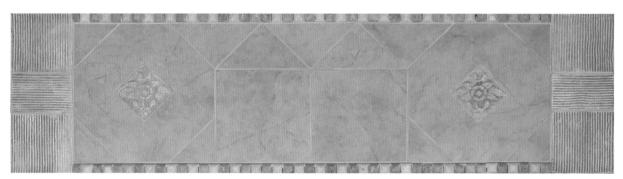

An 18-inch backsplash created with simple beige tile shapes, but this time, we have added texture.

COLOR: THE THIRD DESIGN ELEMENT ✢ Color can create a very noticeable change in any detail concept. Using the same shapes from the first three projects, let's see how color can have an impact on the design.

Project 4 ✢ The use of color tiles makes the individual tile shapes pop, and adds warmth and richness to the basic tile pattern. Notice that the finish of the tiles adds a rustic feel to the backsplash, in contrast to the clean, modern look of the same pattern in Project 1.

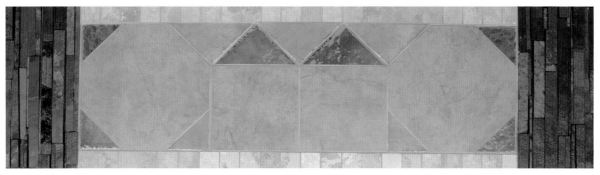

The same 18-inch backsplash concept as in the other examples, but this time added color makes a noticeable difference.

MIXING IT ALL UP: COMBINING DECORATIVE ELEMENTS

Shape, texture, and color are three elements that you can easily use to create decorative details. You can adjust a look a zillion times by simply rearranging each element.

FABRIC DETAILING ✢ Fabric (also known as soft goods) detailing, such as throw pillows, drapes, bedspreads, skirts, and upholstery, also employs the three elements of design. Shape, texture, and color are just as applicable to soft detailing as they are to hard-surface detailing.

Projects 1 to 4 offered tips and techniques for combining shape, color, and texture on tile surfaces. These same techniques can be put to use in fabric. Combining fabrics in a variety of textures can create soft pillows of beauty and distinction. Depending upon the fabric chosen, further decorative details (e.g., trims) may or may not be required.

For purposes of illustration, throw pillows make the perfect medium to demonstrative soft detailing.

Project 5 ✠ One way soft details can be created is through the use of applied materials. In this project, we begin with a purchased, solid color pillow, and create custom details by applying additional fabric pieces and trims, starting by detailing just the face of the pillow, and then by adding decorative borders. (Most detail trims for soft items are purchased. These purchased trims are, in reality, ready-made details.)

We have used all three elements of design in this project: *shape*—the rectangular band in the center of the pillow; *texture*—the rope braid and fringe trim; and *color*—the fabric selections. When detailing soft surfaces, just like hard surfaces, you can adjust a look a zillion times by simply rearranging each element.

1. A basic solid color throw pillow. 2. See how the addition of a fabric band across the center of the plain throw pillow can alter its appearance? You can put this same concept to work on your own store-bought pillows. 3. Now, let's add fabric trim around the edges. See how this small change takes the whole pillow to another level?

4. Our throw pillow with its central fabric band, fabric edge trim, and the newest addition: decorative braid.

5. The final product: the same plain pillow with a central fabric band, fabric edge trim, decorative braid, and fabric fringe. What a difference from the plain pillow we started with!

LARGE-SCALE DECORATIVE DETAILING ✠ In my many years of working with clients, I've learned that the larger the item, the greater the fear of adding decorative detailing. While there is no reason to be afraid of detailing a piece of furniture, the reality is that most people would probably never even think of it, and that would be a shame. I think it's one of the best places to make your personal style statement! Most furniture detailing is on cabinet units, such as entertainment units, most commonly on the doors and drawer fronts.

The same three detail elements that apply to tile and to fabric also apply to furniture pieces:

Shape—Applied moldings
Texture—Hardware
Color—Wood or selected finish

The shapes most commonly used for doors and drawers are rectangular, with the occasional square. Adding new molding and decorative detailing to door and drawer fronts can radically alter the appearance of the cabinetry. These decorative additions can be as simple or as complex as desired. The look can be further enhanced with the addition of texture and color.

Project 6 ✠ Here are some great examples of how to use the three design elements to create widely divergent looks on cabinet doors. Starting with a plain, solid wood door, we first added a simple picture molding around the perimeter. We added more picture molding to the center of the door, adding even more visual depth to the door. The addition of a decorative medallion centered inside the second picture molding adds luxury and a sense of formality to the door. Finally, a deep, burnished stain creates an Old World feel.

1. An unadorned flat-panel wooden cabinet door.

2. The same door with decorative picture molding applied to the edges.

3. A flat-panel door, once double picture molding has been applied.

4. A flat-panel door, once double picture molding and a decorative medallion have been applied.

5. What a difference a little color makes!

THROUGH THE EYES OF CECIL

SEVEN RULES FOR DECORATIVE DETAILING

1. Remind yourself of the original goal for your décor. (It will keep you from getting carried away in the detailing process if your original vision is always fresh in your mind.)

2. Select items that will complement your décor and meet your goals.

3. Try to look at ordinary objects with a different eye—for example, the doors to my dining room buffet have handles made of Ethiopian carved horn spoons. It's always interesting to add a dash of the unexpected!

4. Remember that not every surface or structure requires a decorative detail element. (That would be too much, which is fatal to any décor.) Instead, start by selecting a few areas for detailing and build from there.

5. Details are content to play a supporting role.

6. If you like a detail element, but you're not 100 percent sure, live with it for a while before you make your final decision. In the end, it's really only your opinion that counts.

7. Have fun with the process!

PULLING IT ALL TOGETHER: CREATING A HOME

Your home must be a powerhouse. It has to be your energy source, your inspiration. Today, most of our lives are spent indoors and, for this reason, our homes need to be more of a nurturing environment, and we can look to nature for our inspiration in accomplishing this. After all, nature is an ever-changing collection of colors, textures, and substances—all of which refresh and stimulate the mind. And though we can't change our interiors as often as nature changes its colors, we can find endless design detailing ideas in it.

The home demands details that will keep you excited about your interior environment. A touch of detailing on the floor, walls, ceiling, furnishings, and accessories can give lasting gratification. The decorated room—the sum of all the individual parts—is what brings pleasure and gives happiness. A room with details intrigues the mind, I think because of its singularity.

So, just what is creative detailing, anyway? We all know that it has something to do with decorative ornamentation, but perhaps we're not quite clear on the concept. I think creative detailing can be summarized with these four words: *creative, decorative, ornate,* and *detail.* These definitions from the Merriam-Webster Dictionary also largely define the concept of decorative detailing: *Creative*—having the quality of something imaginative; *Decorative*—serving to decorate; especially something that is purely ornamental; *Ornate*—a synonym for *decorate*; to enhance the appearance . . . especially with beautiful objects; and *Detail*—a part of a whole: as one of the small elements that collectively constitute a work of art.

Each of these definitions has some bearing on my personal definition of creative detailing, which is *the act of adding small touches to your décor to enhance its appearance and to add interest and appeal.* In truth, it's pretty much my definition for adding accessories to my wardrobe, too!

Creative detailing is something that can be added at the planning and installation stages of any décor. The exciting thing, however, is that it can also be added much later in the process—even years later—without creating tremendous problems. If you don't think that's exciting, let me put it another way: You can continue to add decorative detailing to your home as time, and inspiration, allows. Isn't that the most empowering thought? You don't have to get everything perfect right from the start!

My own home is proof positive of this, since I tend to use it as a working laboratory of decorative detailing. I have been adding, removing, even reworking decorative details off and on throughout my fifteen-year residency. (My husband probably wishes I would stop!) Since I am both the designer *and* the client, if I can see something in my mind, I want it in my room. And, of course, I have the luxury of being able to set my own time frame for completing the detail work.

Naturally, I don't have that luxury when working on a client's home: It has to be right on the first installation. I can only imagine myself knocking on the door a year or more later and trying to sell a detail concept after the fact. The conversation might go, "Hello again! Listen, I have just thought of a great detail for your home. I know I finished it last year, but stone on the living room walls would be so perfect. I really think you should consider the idea. I know it's messy, time-consuming, and expensive, but it will truly be worth all the

heartache and pain once it's finished." Yeah, right. I can just see me getting escorted off the premises, too!

Where can you add decorative detailing in your home? Actually, I can't think of anywhere where you *cannot* add it. Detailing is about adding creative touches—often, simple changes (or a series of simple changes)—to an existing décor. These changes can be structural or decorative and involve either hard surfaces (e.g., tile, wood) or soft (e.g., fabric, pillows). Decorative detailing can even involve the arrangement, or rearrangement, of existing accessories. Some areas that could benefit from decorative detailing are:

- ☩ Backsplashes
- ☩ Ceilings
- ☩ Fireplaces
- ☩ Furniture
- ☩ Upholstery
- ☩ Walls
- ☩ Windows

Here's a concept that may not immediately spring to mind: How about adding details to some of the existing decorative elements in the room? I'm talking about items such as throw pillows, lampshades, draperies, bed linens, table linens, etc. In many cases, you can use items you already own, or purchase items with the idea of embellishing them by adding your own decorative elements.

Believe me, once you start thinking about it, you will realize that there are many possibilities. And once you actually begin to implement your ideas, you will be amazed at what you can achieve with just a little decorative detail!

To add character to this home, I opted for decorative detailing in the form of beach paneling on the walls. The room is two stories tall and I used the beach trim detail to tie the three sections together and to extend across the adjacent wall of windows for architectural impact.

LET'S REVIEW

Decorative detailing is the act of adding small touches to your décor to enhance its appearance and to add interest and appeal. These details, which can be applied to endless areas in the home, are made up of three elements: shape, texture/finish, and color. This holds true whether your medium is hard (tile) or soft (pillows).

Decorative details can be added at any stage of a project. Not only can you create the details at the inception of your décor, you can also add them long after your original design was finished. Regardless of when you plan to add decorative details, you want to keep several things in mind:

- ✤ Remind yourself of the original goal for your décor.
- ✤ Make sure to select items that will complement your décor.
- ✤ Look at ordinary objects with a different perspective. (It's always interesting to add a dash of the unexpected!)
- ✤ Remember that not every surface or structure requires a decorative detail element.
- ✤ Details should play a supporting role.
- ✤ Live with your detail element for a while before you make your final decision.
- ✤ Have fun with the process!
- ✤ There is no rule that says you cannot add decorative detailing to purchased items.

About five years after I finished decorating my home for the first time, I had a marvelous design detail idea for a 45-degree angled wall located at the end of the foyer. This wall is only 1½ feet wide but about 16 feet high—quite narrow, and very tall. At the time it was the only angled wall in the entire house, and because I felt that this wall was different for a reason, I wanted it to play up that difference. So, I applied split travertine to the wall. (Split travertine is marble spliced in strips, typically 3 inches wide x 12 inches high. It has a rough texture when unfilled, but a subtle coloration.) This particular split travertine was left over from an earlier installation on the face of my bar, so not only did I feel that it would add subtle texture to the wall, it had the added benefit of being already on hand. (Did I mention that I'm a use-the-leftover-chicken-to-make-chicken-soup type of a gal?) The ultimate result: a subtle change in color and texture, which added up to big benefits in the architectural treatment!

2

FLOORING DETAILS

When you're looking for detail elements, I think that it is important to be creative. For me, that means exploring alternative materials. Personally, I am always seeking products that will give my clients' homes that special look.

FLOORING IS OFTEN overlooked in the search for decorative detailing. I don't know if this is because it comes preinstalled (unless you are building a custom house) or because changing it seems like too much expense. What I do know is that the floor is the foundation for your entire decorative scheme and that adding the right decorative detail can take your décor to new heights!

Usually, most of the floor area is covered with furniture, and hard-surface floors are often detailed with large area rugs. So let's take a moment to talk about the best areas for adding decorative detailing or "accent motifs." Consider these points:

- ⊹ Floor accent details must be in an area that will be noticed, such as the middle of the foyer.
- ⊹ Floor details should not be covered by furniture.
- ⊹ The only exception to the rule above is when the details are small accent details that are part of the total floor design.
- ⊹ Floor details must either balance or outline a space.
- ⊹ The size of floor detail product is important to the finished design.
- ⊹ Floor designs are best planned before installation.
- ⊹ Colors, finishes, and types of floor details can be long-term commitments to your décor, so choose wisely.

Flooring is available in a variety of materials, and there is no hard-and-fast rule for combining materials within an installation. You'll want to keep function and overall design aesthetic in mind. You'll also want to make sure that you keep the floor height level when combining different flooring materials such as tile and wood, carpet and tile, or other combinations—uneven transitions between different flooring materials create tripping hazards. In addition, you should be aware of the cleaning requirements of each material that you plan to install.

In this home, natural limestone is bordered with slab marble. To create definition between the rooms, mosaic limestone tile was installed in the transitional space.

THROUGH THE EYES OF CECIL

Foyers and gallery halls are my favorite areas for adding decorative floor detailing. That's because floor detailing is an eye catcher even without a furniture composition, and it adds design to a space that may have no other décor.

Decorative borders and a figured background in shades of taupe and cream create a carpet that mirrors the decorative wall treatment.

The most common flooring materials available today are:

- Carpets and Rugs
- Ceramic
- Glass
- Leather
- Stone
- Wood

All of them have one thing in common: their unlimited potential for adding style, charm, and decorative appeal.

DETAILING FLOORS WITH CARPETS AND RUGS

Contrary to popular belief, you can create decorative carpet (and rug) details, and you have many options when you do. You can commission a custom weaving, where your design is woven into the carpet on the loom, or you can purchase two or more different ready-made carpets and hire a carver to cut and bind them together.

Wall-to-wall carpeting (and custom-created rugs) can accept decorative detailing in the form of unusual borders, motifs, and color combinations. This decorative detailing concept requires the aid of a professional carpet carver, but it is certainly within the realm of affordability.

Both area rugs and wall-to-wall carpeting come in a variety of materials from natural fibers to man-made, and both are available at many price points. Rugs and carpets come in two grades: commercial and residential. Commercial-grade carpeting is designed for extremely heavy traffic areas and is usually installed without a pad. Residential carpeting, on the other hand, is designed for areas less heavily traveled, and is always installed with a carpet pad.

Personally, when I think of overall area rug or wall-to-wall carpeting installation, I don't automatically think of decorative detailing. (An overall installation is not a decorative detail. Remember, we've defined that as a little additive that enhances the end result.) There is, however, one type of area-rug installation that is, truly, a decorative detail. We're so used to area rugs underfoot that they seem to us to be a natural part of any décor. But, when that area rug—complete with fringe—is actually composed of decorative tile, you have an unusual decorative detail, and one that has always fascinated me! (See decorative-tile rug on page 32.)

DETAILING FLOORS WITH CERAMIC TILE

Ceramic tile is easily accessible, since you can find it in most home-improvement stores. The price point is low, but the colors and patterns are almost endless, and—with finishes from high gloss to matte and textures that range from smooth to rough—ceramic tile can evoke any mood. Because the material is so prevalent, it's not uncommon for the consumer to run across closeouts and one-of-a-kinds on tile. If you see something wonderful, even if there are only a few tiles, I advise you to buy it because, if you love the look, you can use it as a detail.

Custom detailing can be fun! In this living room carved insets of red, purple, and blue create the illusion of trails of colorful paint against a white background.

DETAILING FLOORS WITH GLASS

Glass tile is currently a hot commodity in the design marketplace. With its combination of bright color and reflective surface, it is visually delicious. Glass tile is also versatile: It can be used anywhere that ceramic tile is used. But glass tile is often overlooked as a flooring surface. Contrary to popular belief, glass tile can be used on the floor—I've been doing it for years.

Glass can be expensive but, decoratively speaking, you get a lot of design bang for your buck. If you love the idea of using it, but haven't got a huge budget, glass tile makes a fabulous detail element. There is no danger of glass being overlooked, with its reflective quality. In fact, when used as an inset detail, a small amount of glass tile makes tremendous impact. It's also extremely easy to mix glass tiles with ceramic in your detail concepts because both materials are installed in exactly the same manner. (See glass tile floor on page 159.)

DETAILING FLOORS WITH LEATHER

Leather isn't something that people generally think of when they think of flooring, but it is readily available. It comes in various finishes from flat to tooled (embossed) and can be applied to just about any surface. Leather wears wonderfully, and ultimately develops a rich patina. Floors covered in this manner sound soft, look rich, and feel fabulous underfoot. As an added benefit, these treatments get better and better with the passage of time—just like a favorite pair of shoes or leather jacket.

DETAILING FLOORS WITH METAL

Stainless steel has recently moved into the design marketplace. Intended for use on floors (and walls!), it's available as metal tiles and sheets of textured metal. Probably the easiest way to use the material is in the form of tiles, and these metal tiles are available in many sizes, shapes, and patterns.

The look of metal tile is so strong that I prefer to use it in smaller quantities. Since metal tile, like glass, can be extremely expensive, I prefer to add it as an accent detail to a plan that I have already designed. I always use the metal tile in the size that we order and make sure that I lay it out so that no cutting is necessary. This is important, because metal tile cannot be easily cut—if it can be cut at all.

OPPOSITE ❖ Leather flooring is often an unexpected application in any room. However, over time, the material wears well and develops a rich patina. It is soft underfoot and is a great insulator against noise.

RIGHT ❖ Metal accent tiles have been combined with tumbled marble to create a beautiful and unusual kitchen floor treatment. While 1-inch x 1-inch accent tiles have been inset in the main body of the floor, liner tiles and 4-inch x 4-inch accents have been used to create a fabulous decorative border.

DETAILING FLOORS WITH STONE

I have been using natural stone floorings for a good many years now. For overall flooring, Crema Marfil marble and Saturnia marble are favorites of many of my clients because of the pale color and, when installed, the overall feeling of spaciousness that they convey. I have also used Absolute Black granite and Black Galaxy granite for several installations, mostly in clients' contemporary homes. Absolute Black, like its name implies, is an inky black with absolutely no variation in color throughout. Black Galaxy, on the other hand, is a black stone with small bronze gold sprinkles (hence the name). Either one creates a dramatic base for furnishings and accessories, and an even more dramatic backdrop for design detailing.

RIGHT ✣ I love the concept of a tile "rug." This installation on a brick veranda really makes a statement. Who would have thought that you could get all of the detail of an Oriental carpet, complete with decorative fringe, in a tile installation? I love it!

OPPOSITE ✣ Decorative marble medallion was installed in the center of the flooring to echo the shape of the steps. Inset tiles throughout the floor pick up the motif of the medallion.

THROUGH THE EYES OF CECIL

To make the decision on an accent detail for the floor you may think, "Why does the area look better with it?" In my dining room, I had two Lucite dining-table bases that lost their brightness when placed against the beige tile. By installing the black granite flooring detail, I was able to give luminescence back to the two Lucite table bases. How well did I succeed? Let's just say that every time photos of this room are published, my office is deluged with calls from people who want to buy a table just like it!

In Florida, where I do most of my work, tile seems to be the flooring material of choice. For that reason, I don't often get asked to install wood flooring. One couple, however, decided to be different. Not only did they want wood, they wanted inlaid wood in their foyer. In this case, we used maple for the ground material and walnut as the accent, which resulted in a pleasing contrast. The design itself is a linear checkerboard design. This straightforward application, which was the work of a master craftsman, was inlaid by hand at the job site and is used to delineate the foyer area.

DETAILING FLOORS WITH WOOD

Wood flooring is available in two forms: planks and tiles (parquet), and, in several types: solid wood, engineered wood flooring, and pseudo-wood. Wood floors add warmth and an element of nature to an environment, and they can be detailed fairly easily.

Wood floors are sealed, often with varnish or polyurethane, which comes in matte, satin, and high-gloss finishes. They are easy to care for: daily dusting and weekly wet mopping (with water only; no cleansers or polishes, they strip or dull the finish) keep them sparkling clean.

If the look appeals to you, it's now possible to find prefabricated wood inlay designs especially for flooring. This can save you time and money. But if it's a truly custom design that you need, the master craftsman is still your best recourse.

I love to install contrasting colored tiles in the foyers of my clients' homes. I am particularly proud of this installation, which involves the use of four different varieties in one stunning whole.

COMBINING MULTIPLE FLOORING MATERIALS

Decorative flooring details can be created through the juxtaposition of multiple materials, as I mentioned above. Even if you want to keep to the same type of material (e.g., stone) throughout the floor, it is still possible to combine varieties of that one material into striking and unusual decorative details. You could combine polished and unpolished stone (in similar or dissimilar colors) or use different types of stone (granite and marble, for example).

You can also create unique combinations with glass tile insets, wood with ceramic tile insets, wood with metal tile accents, or stone or ceramic tile with carpeting, just to cite a few of the many possible combinations. Make sure these decorative details are installed level with the overall floor—you don't want decorative details that are higher (or lower) than the majority of your floor surface because it's unsafe (tripping hazards) and it would also be difficult to keep clean. It's okay to be creative; you just have to be knowledgeable about the products you choose.

USING CONTRASTING COLORS TO CREATE DESIGN DETAILS

One of the most obvious decorative detail concepts (at least to me) involves the use of contrasting color. It's perfectly possible to employ this concept whether you are working with natural stone flooring, ceramic tile, linoleum, glass, or even wood. Black on white or white on black makes for drama, but materials are available in all color ranges, should you choose to go for something less stark in appearance.

Another option, at least when working with tile, is to use colored grout. Often I will combine white or cream-colored ceramic tile with gray grout. It makes a subtle design detail and has the added benefit of ease of maintenance. Keeping white grout "white" is a time-consuming proposition—ask anyone!

When creating decorative detail concepts for your floors, you are really limited only by your imagination.

The addition of small black insets in the tile floor provide interest and pick up the color of the wrought-iron balustrade.

LET'S REVIEW

Flooring is often overlooked as a surface for decorative detailing. Since it is always seen with your interior décor, however, it's one area where the unexpected can have significant impact. Of all the materials available for flooring, most are available as tiles of one size or another. When creating your decorative detail concepts, keep the following in mind:

- ✤ Overall design aesthetic
- ✤ Traffic conditions
- ✤ Durability of material(s) under consideration
- ✤ Cleaning requirements
- ✤ Compatibility of materials (especially important if you are combining very different materials)

Some potential concepts for decorative flooring details:

- ✤ Adding contrasting borders—either color or material—around the edge of the room
- ✤ Decorative material insets—especially suitable for expensive options (e.g., glass or metal)
- ✤ Medallions and other decorative inlays
- ✤ Unusual or arresting combinations of shapes

In this entry foyer, inset tile creates the decorative detail. Here I used a combination of metal tiles and contrasting granite to create the detail. The predominant flooring material is Black Galaxy granite, with contrasting gray granite and metal tiles in the decorative medallion.

WALL AND TRIM DETAILS

There are two indisputable facts about walls, both of which you can use to your advantage. First, walls are covered with something—e.g., paint, wallpaper, fabric. Second, that covering can be just about any product. If it doesn't cut, scratch, or bite, and you can clean it, you can use it to detail a wall.

WALLS PROVIDE A perfect canvas to showcase decorative details. That's because you can't get away from them: You will always see the walls as part of the overall composition of a room or set of rooms. Details and designs have the ability to pull everything all together and provide you with a one-of-a-kind look, so you want to be very careful to keep the finished goal in mind. All good designs (and this includes creative details and installations) begin with a plan.

- ✠ *Determine the style you desire.* Ask yourself: Is my style formal or informal? Is my décor easily identifiable as a certain period or style (e.g., Victorian, French Provincial)? Is the detail being used for theme purposes (such as in a game room or child's bedroom)?
- ✠ *Select material suitable for your installation.* Ask yourself: Who will be the primary occupants of the space? How will the space be used? Are there any special requirements for the space? Once you have this information, you can move forward and select the material(s) to use.
- ✠ *Determine how to install your detail.* Ask yourself: Am I planning to install it myself? Can I really handle the job? Can I make it look like it was professionally installed? Be honest. It has been my experience that a great many concepts fail in the installation phase. Make a realistic assessment of your skills and hire a professional if you think that the installation might be too much for you to handle. It's better to spend a little more on the installation than to waste your entire design concept (not to mention budget) with mediocre execution.

For this client, I used sandblasted glass panels on one wall in his living room/foyer. This unusual wall treatment connects directly with an adjacent custom-created water feature, which uses both glass and stainless steel elements.

TRADE SECRET

There are many materials that can be used to add decorative touches to your walls. Among them are:

- ✤ Fabric
- ✤ Metal*
- ✤ Mirror/glass*
- ✤ Molding*
- ✤ Paint
- ✤ Stone*
- ✤ Tile
- ✤ Wallpaper
- ✤ Wood*

Any or all of these materials can be used to create detail treatments. I have used each of them at one time or another to create decorative details and accents. Items denoted with an asterisk (*) are those that I have also used to detail in place of wall art.

DETAILING WALLS WITH MOLDING

These shaped lengths of wood, plaster, stone, etc. are designed to give ornament to a room, surface, or a piece of furniture, and are often used to conceal joints between one building surface and another, or to give added prominence to a special feature or architectural element. Molding comes in various sizes and shapes. It also comes in dozens of standard profiles—the profile is the design that is cut into the face of the wood—most of which are readily available. Whatever you propose, there is a molding perfect for you.

One of the best arguments for using molding in your decorative concepts is that it can easily be added after the fact, once you have had time to live with your décor for a bit. That's the beauty of creating decorative details with this treatment! Molding is available in the following materials: architectural foam, glass, metal, rubber/resin, stone, wood, plaster, and other materials.

BANG-FOR-YOUR-BUCK APPEAL ✤ Most of the molding details that follow are defined by the use of either carved relief molding or picture framing materials. These two products offer endless possibilities for creativity and I tend to use them to create that one-of-a-kind look. I discovered these products in the course of designing (and manufacturing) custom furnishings for my clients, but I now also use these luscious moldings to add special details to any flat surface that will accept them. It is my belief that adding carved molding to an interior element adds sculptural artistry to the décor.

Remember that you are not limited to the stock moldings in your home-improvement store. There many options, and I suggest that you explore possibilities! Sometimes you will find that the most unexpected alternative—for instance, carved picture frame molding—is the one that will have the most impact. It may cost a little bit more initially, but it will make all the difference to the design. Overall this application is a "10" when it comes to bang-for-your-buck appeal.

DRESSING UP WITH MOLDING ⊹ I think we've all seen that big, boring box of a room and wondered what to do to liven it up. (In fact, it's the number one décor-related question that I hear from family and friends.) I tend to use molding to address this issue.

Crown Molding ⊹ One way to add character to the basic box room is to install crown molding as part of your decorative detail concept. This molding usually runs completely around a room at the point where the wall and the ceiling come together. (Traditionally, crown molding is the name given to a particular profile of molding. But, with all the different types of molding available today, there is no reason why you can't install whatever profile suits your taste.)

Crown molding is often combined with other moldings to create complex wall treatments, and it is not difficult to install. The tricky part is cutting it so that the corners meet properly. To solve this problem, decorative blocks may be used in combination with crown molding. These blocks, which are available at home-improvement centers, are designed to be installed directly into the corner areas of the room and eliminate the need for mitered corner cuts and tedious fitting of crown molding. Of course, you can also create your own corner blocks, as we have done in our office.

In one of my latest home installations, the wall-to-wall vanity mirror in the master bath is framed out with molding. It's an unusual application that looks and feels unquestionably rich.

THROUGH THE EYES OF CECIL

Crown molding comes in standard widths of between 4 and 6 inches. If you choose to install this trim, take note of the ceiling height. The basic rule of thumb is the higher the wall, the wider the crown molding, although you probably don't want to use anything that is less than 4 inches wide. You can also install more than one molding to create the illusion of a wider trim. The choice is yours!

In my office I used a carved picture frame molding with a floral design highlighted with gold leaf in place of traditional crown molding. A rich look, this molding is an upgrade from typical profile molding, which is stain or paint grade.

Suppose that you have a wall that doesn't quite reach the ceiling. Can you add crown molding to it without it looking out of place? Of course you can! In one client's home I did just that, installing a 6-inch-wide egg-and-dart molding to finish off a divider wall between the living room and the kitchen. This wall stops a good 6 feet short of the 14-foot ceiling, but the molding still looks right at home. That's because this wall is recessed 12 inches between two columns, so it has a natural starting and stopping point, which makes a difference when you are adding trim to only one wall or section within a room. (Note: If there is no natural stopping point, the application looks unfinished.) I used a black walnut stain on the molding and highlighted it with a gold rub to create an unusual and commanding decorative detail.

Custom Molding ✤ You can also create your own custom molding for decorative detailing. A simple way to customize molding is to combine two or more ready-made molding profiles together to create your own original look. You can also make your own moldings from scratch (the possibilities are limited only by your skill level and your tools.) If you don't feel you have the ability to make your own, take your ideas to a carpenter or cabinetmaker for execution.

THROUGH THE
EYES OF CECIL

When I know my clients are not art

collectors, I get busy visualizing a wall

design that requires little or no art at all. My

material of choice is molding or panel material

that has texture.

Originally, this living room was a large square room with plenty of space for living but lacking in architectural details. To add charm, I added a large, custom molding made of ¾-inch-thick white oak. We built the frame, designed to resemble a grate, to our requirements and then added vertical members equally spaced about 2 inches apart. Once it was installed, the peek-a-boo spaces allowed the wall surface to become part of the design. This installation epitomizes the ease with which decorative molding can be used.

The chair rail detail in this home is created with molding, but it is not wood molding. It is actually stone tile molding in a rope shape, which was glued directly to the drywall above the wainscot treatment. The wainscot detailing is created with maple wood with inlaid walnut molding strips. The three-dimensional wood squares, which have been applied on the diagonal, add another dimension to this treatment. Faux finishing is used to make the outlet cover blend into the half wall of maple wood.

I love decorative baseboard treatments, but there is nothing that says it has to be limited to standard builder's molding. In this case, the baseboard is stone tile topped with a 1-inch decorative wooden molding, a one-of-a-kind baseboard treatment.

Frame Molding ✥ Molding can be used to add dimension to flat, plain walls. A frame made of molding can highlight what you hang: art, faux murals, mirror, wallpaper, or fabric. This treatment takes its cue from beautifully framed art and is a classic look. Not only does it add dimension and texture to the walls, it makes the display area much more pronounced. So, if your artwork budget is not large, consider adding decorative molding to the wall. It's a great way to add prominence to a small piece of art.

A feature wall is usually the first wall one sees when entering a room, and it is an excellent area for decorative detailing to be added to emphasize something that is already prominent. In bedrooms, the feature wall is always the bed wall, and over the course of my career I have designed many stunning feature walls for this purpose.

Chair Rail Molding ✥ When you need to create the illusion of an enlarged space, I suggest using chair rail moldings. This horizontally applied molding, originally designed to protect plaster walls from damage inflicted by chairs, visually elongates a space. It can be used alone or in conjunction with other elements and is often paired with paint or wallpaper treatments. Chair rail is also often an integral part of wainscot treatments. To me, chair rail is a detail baseboard that has risen to greater heights. Consider using this horizontal detail in a flat room. It will customize the room beyond belief.

ADDING PIZZAZZ WITH MOLDING ✥ I've used wallpaper as part of the installations in several clients' homes, covering entire rooms, feature walls, and architectural details. But when you set wallpaper off with molding, it is elevated to artful design detailing. Here's a technique I've used in several homes throughout the years: Take an allover decorative wallpaper treatment and augment it with molding for decorative appeal.

Baseboard Molding ✥ It doesn't matter if your home is worth thousands, hundreds of thousands, or millions of dollars: Upgrade your baseboard. Although it seems like a small detail, adding a 5- to 6-inch-wide baseboard of paint-grade wood will upgrade any home, and it doesn't require taking out a second mortgage. I'm speaking from personal experience here. In my own home we replaced the original builder-installed base with one of solid walnut that is 6 inches high. A small change, it may seem, but one that has had lasting impact on the décor. In a nutshell, that is what detailing is all about!

Clever use of molding can relieve the necessity for art, which is illustrated in my client's living room and dining room areas, where we used molding as a replacement for artwork. To do this we first added the chair rail. Next, we installed molding in the form of wooden "frames." Above the chair rail we added large molding frames, and beneath the rail, small frames were added for balance. The same trim molding, although smaller in scale, was also added above the stone baseboard. Large-scale molding was added to the individual ceiling "trays" in the coffered ceiling treatment. Finally, for continuity we added molding at the top of the column, which divides the living and dining rooms.

In this lovely master bedroom, it's hard to tell just what the accent treatment is. Is it the textured wallpaper I used on the headboard wall, the simple vertical molding treatment, or the dental molding used in place of traditional crown molding? Actually, it's the vertical molding because it draws attention to the headboard wall.

I love using vertical molding in an installation. It's especially effective when paired with textured wallpaper.

OPPOSITE ✥ Recently, I created a feature wall in this bedroom, which displays panels of faux leather, framed out by three-step silver leaf picture framing. I also used the picture framing to divide the panels on the wall. This picture framing is now a major component in an innovative wall treatment!

THROUGH THE EYES OF CECIL

Using a mixture of materials in decorative detailing is just as easy as mixing them in your attire. It's a fact that when we are fully clothed, we are truly a walking mix of textures. Leather shoes, fabric garments, metal jewelry, plastic eyewear (or credit cards!), straw hat, etc. You mix it up on your body every day, so don't let the concept intimidate you at home. Even though your wall is larger, it certainly can carry off a mix of textures. Why not give it a try? Mixed media can change the ordinary into something special. Everyone expects wood molding as the top trim or chair rail treatment, but I like to look for unexpected elements to create the "wow!" factor.

THROUGH THE EYES OF CECIL

There are four things to consider when using baseboard as an accent:

- the material (e.g., wood, stone)
- the height
- the profile
- the finish (e.g., paint, stain, faux finish, etc.)

DETAILING WALLS WITH WALLPAPER, FAUX FINISHES, AND PAINT

Wallpaper, faux finishes, and paint have been used on walls for centuries to create beautiful interior designs. As decorative detail elements, however, they are also powerful tools. Creating decorative details with any one of these treatments means using them to adorn existing interior elements. If you want more information on using paint as part of an overall interior design, please see my previous book, *9 Steps to Beautiful Living: Dream, Design, and Decorate Your Home with Style*.

As decorative detail elements, wallpaper, faux finishes, and paint can be used to bring pattern, texture, and color to a wall, to add borders, to create window treatments, to add decorative accents, and to make disparate items blend together, among other options.

BRINGING PATTERN, PEXTURE, AND COLOR TO THE WALL ✠ Adding color as part of a detail element can be as simple as painting or faux finishing an accent wall. In several homes, I have used partial-height walls as an accent to the overall décor. In most instances these walls are specifically placed to screen portions of the clients' interior space. Regardless of this, they are a prominent part of the decorative design. The challenge is creating a decorative finish, which harmonizes with the surrounding décor while at the same time playing up the design detail. Personally, I like to use subtle paint treatments as part of this process. I often partner faux finishes with architectural elements in my clients' homes because I believe that it adds additional interest.

THROUGH THE EYES OF CECIL

Whenever you faux finish a wall or series of walls, I recommend that you extend the finish to the outlet covers and switch plates. This small step serves to make them vanish right before your eyes!

For this client, I added a stepped partial wall treatment. This tone-on-tone paint treatment features neutral colors arranged in a square design. The treatment accents the tiered wall, which divides the dining room and the dinette.

DETAILING WALLS WITH METAL

Mention metal as a decorative material, and most people tend to think of ceiling tile, if they think of anything at all. But in reality there are many types of metal that can be used for decorative detailing, and all of them can be applied to the wall. These range from the old-fashioned tin ceiling tile, to metal laminates, metal moldings, metal tiles, and even textured sheet metals.

TIN-TYPE APPEAL ✛ Metal ceiling tile has been around since the Victorian age, and this product is still readily available. But did you know that it can be a great detail application for walls, and backsplashes, in addition to the ceiling? Nowadays, metal is usually available in sheets as opposed to individual tiles. It's lightweight and can be cut to size with tin snips (although protective gloves should be worn since the metal edges are sharp and you can easily get cut), making this a great product for the DIY enthusiast.

LAMINATED METAL AS A DECORATIVE DETAIL ✛ Another great wall product is laminate metal, which consists of thin-gauge metal laminated to a thin backing. Laminate metal is easy to install since it can be cut with a hobby saw and then glued into place with construction adhesives. Unlike thick-gauge metal, laminate metals can be smoothed around the edges with sandpaper with just a little effort, making accidental cuts less likely. When you combine laminated metal panels and wood molding on a single wall, you get a wall with drama and dimension. Metal laminates, used alone or mixed with other materials, provide dramatic backdrops for paintings and other art. I highly recommend this product, not only for its ease of installation, but also for its versatility.

The materials selected for this contemporary living room include 10-inch x 48-inch stainless steel-embossed laminated panels and Japanese ash molding; the panels are affixed onto the wall and framed out with the Japanese ash. The wall treatment complements the silver faux finish and Japanese ash columns in the dining room area. The look is strong and bold, but not too bold to accept three abstract paintings.

THROUGH THE EYES OF CECIL

Baseboard of all types is best installed *after* the installation of hard-surface floors such as stone, tile, or wood. This is because stone and tile floors are set in mud, which can be extremely messy and damaging to preinstalled baseboard, but which will also raise the floor height by as much as 2 to 3 inches. Conversely, this means that you may lose 2 to 3 inches from the height of your baseboard. Hard-surface floors are also completely rigid. When your hard-surface floor abuts preinstalled baseboard, the baseboard becomes sealed in place, making it nearly impossible to remove. This also holds true for hardwood flooring installations. Baseboard in carpeted areas is best installed *before* the carpet is laid. That's because carpet is installed with tack strips or glue. When baseboard is installed at floor height it may not be a straight, even line on the wall, the reason being that many floor foundations are uneven. Carpet installers can raise the level of the floor with wood or concrete to allow the carpet and the base to meet perfectly every time.

THROUGH THE EYES OF CECIL

Mirror is a common fixture in bathrooms; you can find it just about anywhere. In my eyes, however, adding trim around the mirror makes for a great wall detail.

DETAILING WALLS WITH MIRROR, GLASS, AND PLASTIC LAMINATES

I am a great believer in always being on the lookout for new design materials and applications. There are so many products that can be used in decorative detailing available on the market, that one or another of them will change your mind about wall covering if you let it. While mirror, glass, and plastic laminates serve practical, utilitarian purposes, they are also surprisingly beautiful and versatile materials to use in decorative detailing.

DECORATIVE DETAILS WITH MIRROR ✣ I like to use mirror in many applications. Generally, I use it to visually increase the size of a space. I often, however, also use it to flood more light into an area. I really love mirror's reflective qualities, particularly when it's used in combination with glass accessories.

DECORATIVE DETAILS WITH GLASS ✣ The typical glass design details are windows and glass accessories. But glass can be used to great effect on (or in) walls, so let your imagination run wild. Glass is available in many thicknesses and colors, can be cut to just about any size, and its edges can be sanded or beveled.

In my own work, Rudy Art Glass Studio was an exciting find for me. The company specializes in laminated glass and can combine any one of the following to clear, textured, and stained glass: light diffusing and color inter-layers, etching, wire, fabric, graphics, and reverse-paintings. Any or all of these can be used to create products that suit your exact needs. This custom work is expensive, however, so you may want to limit how much you use it in your installation.

OPPOSITE ✣ There's a lot going on in this small powder bath. I used mirror, with added red painted glass to frame it, to visually expand the size of the room. The remaining walls were faux finished to look like blocks, and small 1-inch wooden squares were faux finished and glued to the surface at various points throughout the room. Finally, wall sconces augment the recessed hi-hat lighting.

In this transitional bedroom, the wall finish echoes the windowpane check on the client's upholstered headboard and duvet. To achieve this look, mirrored wall panels, sliver mica wallpaper, black lacquer trim, and decorative silver leaf molding were installed.

There have been times in my professional life when I have had to create a detail to save an installation. Such is the case with this fabulous wall treatment. The wallpaper I selected is called "Beadazzled," and its surface is composed of small glass beads, which looked lovely in my studio. After it was installed on the 20-foot-high wall, however, the seams were more noticeable than the luster of the paper. I was frantic! The job was not only saved, it was also enhanced by the use of metal. Narrow metal strips were applied to cover the seams, and the juxtaposition of the two elements was all that I could have wished for. This is one decorative detail, however, that I can't take full credit for. My husband, and business partner, found the metal molding and suggested its application here. Now I don't know if he was motivated by the word *Honey* (as in "Sweetheart, could you . . . ?") or *money* (as in "How much would we lose if this installation does not work out?"), but regardless of the motivation, his suggestion really pulled the whole thing together.

TRADE SECRET

This contemporary kitchen has clean lines and a sleek, sophisticated style, which is accented by its sizzling backsplash. The owner, who is a professionally trained chef, had very definite ideas about what he wanted to achieve. The custom-designed kitchen and professional-grade appliances are enhanced by black-and-gray granite countertops and further accented by the red painted-glass backsplash. To achieve the look, silver metallic paint is applied to the underside of the glass. Painted glass, unlike glass tile, has few, if any, seams or grout lines. Talk about a showstopper! Wow!

THE POWER OF PLASTIC LAMINATES ✤ For most people, plastic laminate means Formica. After a bit of research, however, I found a product that is the Rolls-Royce of plastic laminates, which is called Mirroflex. It is a high-impact plastic with a decorative top surface in laminate form. I was intrigued. It couldn't be all that and a bag of chips, could it? Well, after I received a sample of this material, I knew that it was.

THROUGH THE EYES OF CECIL

I can't see a TV as a feature design element; it just doesn't work for me. Now that plasma TVs are the "in" thing, however, I have redirected my entertainment wall units to wall-panel design concepts.

My philosophy for this design was: "If you plan to hang a large plasma TV on a large wall, you ought to make the entire wall a viewing pleasure." So, that is what I set out to do. To achieve the look, Mirroflex laminate was applied to eight ¾-inch plywood panels. Then, a black matte-finished laminate was applied to the four edges of each panel. The wall on which the panels were installed was painted with black matte paint. The gray Mirroflex panels were spaced ¾ of an inch apart, allowing the black paint on the wall to act as a grid. The black-and-gray color scheme was inspired by the black face of the TV and the steel finish of the TV frame.

TRADE SECRET

DETAILING WALLS WITH CERAMIC TILE

Today, ceramic tiles are available in nearly limitless varieties of textures, finishes, colors, sizes, shapes, and designs, and can work in any home from ethnic to traditional to urban modern. Ceramic tiles are so prevalent that it's not uncommon for the general consumer to run across closeouts and other sales on tile. If you come across something wonderful, even if there are only a few tiles, I advise you to buy them. If you love the tile, you can always come up with a detail treatment for your inspirational purchase. Believe me, I've done it!

MOSAIC TILE TECHNIQUES ✚ I consider mosaic a technique not a material, although technically I suppose you could argue that it is a specialized type of tile. (The term Mosaic tile generally refers to tile that is anything less than 2.4-inches square, with 1-inch square being most common). The classic mosaic technique, which involves creating a composition by inlaying small pieces of various materials together to create a design, is age-old. In the ancient world, the most commonly used materials were glass and stone. Today, however, ceramic mosaic tile is the material of choice for the beginner.

Free-form Mosaic ✚ What I call "free-form mosaic," to differentiate it from classic mosaic (as described above), is created from irregularly sized and, often, irregularly shaped pieces of tile in various colors, textures, and materials. You can further embellish a free-form mosaic installation with the addition of

For the accent on the tub in my master bath I used tile to visually break the height of the tub front and to add decorative interest. The tile materials selected were actually a collection of throwaway granite and stone pieces, which I recycled into this beautiful bathroom.

cut or broken materials, or even metal. In one kitchen backsplash installation that I have even seen, cutlery and cooking utensils were applied as part of the mosaic treatment!

DETAILING WITH TILE IN BATH AND POWDER ROOMS ✤ Baths are one of the areas in a home that scream for tile details. (In fact, most of us commonly think of ceramic tile when we think of the bath or powder room.) You can use tile details on the walls and floors, in the shower and tub areas, on the vanity, around mirrors—the list goes on and on. In this hardworking room, a spot of tile here or a line there can really perk up the space.

DETAILING WITH TILE IN KITCHENS ✤ Kitchen areas are another favorite space for tile details. Countertops, backsplashes, flooring, even large range hoods are excellent places for creative touches to complement your décor. For something a little out of the ordinary, how about using tile on the cabinetry to accent flat door panels? Then again, maybe you could inset tile details over the sink or cooktop for a little added pizzazz or to pick up additional detail elements.

With beautiful detailing, even a workspace can become a fun space! The idea that the hood of a cooktop is just a venting source for smoke and grease couldn't be further from the truth. A large hood in the center of the kitchen is just asking for special decorative treatment—in this case, tile. Tile is the perfect material to adorn hoods. It accepts heat and is easy to clean.

The tile accents in a guest bathroom actually started with some leftover liner tiles (1½ inches x 8 inches) in red and green. I had just enough of them to outline the ceiling area of the walls. The remaining tiles were purchased from my local home-improvement store. The 4-inch x 4-inch green-and-red tiles are what is commonly called Builder's Special—mass-produced, inexpensive tile—but in this case with a rich color that creates a fabulous overall impression. This is the type of tile that you find in fast-food restaurants. As you can see, the finished detail is very attractive. Who would have guessed that it all started with some leftover tile bound for the dumpster?

Glass tile in harvest colors of pumpkin, rust, gold, and brown adds character to this kitchen and harmonizes beautifully with the lacquer finish of the cabinetry and stone counter tops. Note the use of the 1-inch x 1-inch mosaic tile on the kitchen island. The transparent glass on the smaller tiles is a subtle foil for the richer tones of the opaque 4-inch x 4-inch wall tiles.

TRADE SECRET

Keep in mind that bottles and drinking glasses can be cut or broken for three-dimensional glass details. What about glass rocks or marble glass beads? Why not? If you can clean it (and glue it of course), use it in free form or porcelain mosaic techniques!

In this client's kitchen the inspiration for the decorative tile treatment came from the wallpaper, which is a creamy beige color adorned with motifs of flowers and spices. Custom-painted tile picks up the floral and spice motif but applies it to a white ceramic tile. A ceramic accent tile of twisted rope and a bull-nose trim the edges of the range hood. The custom tile is carried over onto the backsplash.

DETAILING WITH TILES TO CREATE THE UNEXPECTED ✣ If you think that tile is only for bathroom and kitchen walls, think again. Tiles can be used in the most surprising places including on walls and partial walls, on furniture or staircases, and to decorate or emphasize architectural details.

DETAILING WALLS WITH STONE

People have used stone as a design material for millennia. But these days, you don't have to use it in its raw, found form. All types of stone—from marble to limestone to granite—are available in many forms (slabs, tiles, loose) and in many finishes. While stone can be a cool, or reflective surface, many varieties add warmth, texture, and depth to your décor.

I love stone, and have for years, so it's really exciting for me when I have a client who loves it just as much as I do! Then I get a chance to really go overboard and create something totally unexpected.

STONE AS ART ✣ Stone has such artistic appeal that I have been known to mount a slab of it on the wall as both a detail concept and a work of art in and of itself. It makes a very bold and striking statement.

TRADE SECRET

If your installation requires extensive cutting (i.e., requires a wet saw), my advice is to create the design of your detail area and then hire a professional for the actual installation.

I created a tile headboard for a client that was a major component of the master bedroom feature wall. I used unfilled limestone tile in two different sizes to create my design. First, 12-inch x 12-inch tile was cut and shaped for the top portion of the 6-foot-high headboard. This was then joined to 4-inch x 4-inch limestone tile installed on the diagonal. The transition between the two tiles was accented by a cherry-stained wood detail. At the height of the backrest, the stone adjoins an upholstered panel. The entire installation was then bordered with a stone compound, bull-nose trim with a profile. In this installation, the stone tile creates decorative detailing for both wall and furniture piece, and definitely makes a statement!

DETAILING WALLS WITH WOOD

There are four very good reasons why I love details created with wood: (1) wood can be used to cover over any wall texture; (2) it "fits" in with any style of design; (3) it is a natural material, and its richness doesn't overpower a room; and (4) it can be a unifying element in a décor. From structural columns to ceiling to baseboards to floor, wood can be the perfect choice for any decorative design element.

PANELED WALLS ✤ The rich look of wood can be enjoyed in any room of the home. Gone are the days when its use was restricted to the library or the den. There's no need to limit yourself or your imagination anymore. Achieving full wall coverage with wood is not as difficult as one may think, and even a small amount of wood, when applied to a wall in this manner, is strong enough to create a rich, inviting interior.

Various types of wood applied to a plywood backing are available. Usually these are veneers laminated to panels approximately 8 to 10 feet high and 4 feet wide. (Since most ceilings are 8 to 10 feet high, the size of the wood panels makes for easy installation.) These panels can be either glued or nailed in place and then finished as desired. At this stage of the installation, there will be a series of vertical joints evident on the walls. Additional details—either wood or accent trims—can be added over the vertical joints in order to conceal them and finish off the installation. All in all, it's a fairly simple process, and one that I think only enhances a room.

REWORKING AN EXISTING INTERIOR WITH WOOD ✤ As an interior designer, I am often asked to rework interior spaces. It's simply part of the job. It's not often, however, that I get to rework one of my own. Generally, my repeat clients are buying new (to them) homes and I am redesigning these homes to suit my clients' tastes. So, it's really interesting to see your own work after a space of years and see it again with fresh eyes.

There's sure to be an area in your own home that is the perfect candidate for the balancing touch of wood. Sometimes it may be difficult to visualize, often because you are so used to seeing your walls the same old way. Detailing is about viewing your surroundings in a different light, and often takes some time to develop. Don't get discouraged if it takes hours, even weeks, to discover such a special area.

One of the most dramatic examples of my stone detailing is composed of several different stones shading from light to dark, and mounted above my client's staircase. In this home, the interior décor is predominantly neutral with dark brown and black accents. The decorative detailing provided by the stone collage makes a striking focal point in the entry when seen against the white walls and creamy marble flooring.

THROUGH THE
EYES OF CECIL

To direct my thinking, I always look to the
room to inspire my thoughts. Windows often
are the inspiration for creative interior installations. I also often use them to create balance
in my design concepts.

Wood paneling at chair rail height is a winner whenever you seek to enrich a room. In this living room, maple wood with a walnut wood accent
acts as the backdrop for the living room setting. The maple wall is topped with a stone trim tile of rope design. The wall design can be viewed
as an art wall, since it combines an art niche for the client's wooden sculptures and wall space to display an original oil painting. The chair rail
panels and maple wood cornice frame in the art and make it a focal point.

I've always felt that my design awareness and creative application gets better with time. This belief was recently tested when former clients came to me with a new design commission. Years previously, I had completed their original home. It was a wonderful collaborative effort with all the trimmings, and both my clients and I loved it. Now, they were asking me to redesign and redecorate their home, but in a completely different style.

Per the clients' desire years back, the original layout focused the furniture in the open living and family rooms into one conversational grouping. Now, the clients wanted make each space separate—the living room to be more formal and to allow for conversation, and the family room to be informal and used primarily for TV viewing. The open floor plan, however, remained the driving force in dictating the layout.

One of the first things that I noticed was that the far wall of the great room was really a series of large glass doors bisected by two narrow walls. The room itself features a 14-foot ceiling and, with the large expanse of glass, could make for a cold, uninviting space. I wanted the new layout to play up this element. So, in the new design, I opted to add a touch of wood to provide balance and warmth to the wall area.

THROUGH THE EYES OF CECIL

The use of wood panels with decorative inlays to adorn walls first caught my eye in commercial applications. When I am in a well-designed commercial space, I don't just sit about or wait in lines. I look for details that inspire me!

This bar wall in my client's home is actually the back wall of the kitchen. The towering columns house both the structural supports and the flue for the range hood. The wooden panels visually connect all the elements together and, because it's a natural material, it fits in with the style of the remainder of the room.

I tend to like fabric on walls when it has an

upholstered look—i.e., slightly padded. Flat glue

on applications often looks like wallpaper.

Not long ago, I completed a job where

every room of the home was just right,

except—the master bedroom. My clients were

more than happy, but I knew it wasn't what it

could be. They paid me for my work and left

town for two weeks. During their absence, I

had a vision—upholster the bedroom walls.

The idea wouldn't leave me in peace. I

absolutely had to do it . . . and, before the

clients returned.

I applied foam rubber onto ¼-inch thick

plywood panels (for dimension), then wrapped

fabric around the panels, and finally glued the

panels to the wall. They finished the master

bedroom to perfection. I was overjoyed when

my clients loved their surprise!

DETAILING WALLS WITH FABRIC

Fabric is the most pliable substance imaginable, which makes it a dream to use as a decorative detail. You can sew it, glue it, staple it, cut it with scissors, and otherwise generally manipulate it into any size, shape, or form you desire. That's what makes it such a perfect decorative detail! It's also lightweight, easily handled, and as little as a yard of fabulous fabric can go a long way to energize any décor! That makes fabric *the* decorative material for the handy do-it-yourselfer!

Installing fabric on the wall can create a wonderful design detail. It can also create a maintenance issue, so choose both the area to be upholstered and the material with care. I've used this technique frequently over the years, generally in bedrooms. On the plus side, it allows you to use sumptuous fabrics like silk, linen, even velvet for one-of-a-kind appeal. On the minus side, the more exotic the fabric, the more difficult it is to maintain.

Most of the photographs in this section feature the upholstered panel technique, which I prefer to use because it gives dimension to the wall as a detail treatment. One thing you will notice is that I don't use fabric as a full-coverage technique. Instead, I partner fabric with other materials to create more varied decorative detailing.

Fabric can be applied on walls by using one of four techniques:

- Install like traditional wallpaper
- Staple directly to the wall
- Upholstered wall panels
- Tack-strip technique

Each method has its pros and cons. Whichever one you select will depend upon many factors including, but not limited to, the material selected, the ease of proposed installation, the confidence of the handyman (or ma'am), the experience level of the professional installer, etc. One of these processes will likely appeal to you.

UPHOLSTERED WALL PANELS ⁜ I have been using upholstered wall panels since the early 1980s with phenomenal results, and can say for a fact that I have used this technique more than any other "fabric to wall" application. These panels can be installed to cover either the entire wall space or a portion of it, whichever you choose. Originally, I applied them most often in bedrooms because I believe that look works well there. Nowadays, however, I am also using this treatment to soundproof home theaters because acoustical fabrics not only control sound, but can also be manipulated to make great wall designs.

Usually the first wall one sees when entering a room (the feature wall) is an excellent area to add decorative detailing. In the case of this bedroom, I created a contemporary headboard wall with pearlized vinyl panels, stainless steel, and lacquered wood moldings.

DE-EMPHASIZING EXISTING DOORS

We're all familiar with the old magician's line, "Now you see it, now you don't!" Did you know that you could put that concept to work for you in your own home? It's the case of the vanishing door.

The first thing to know about concealing an interior door on a feature wall is that you start by selecting a covering that is suitable for both the door and the space adjacent to the door. A solid wall and a solid door can accept most materials (e.g., wallpaper, wood, fabric) A door adjacent to a large glass opening should be made of, or covered with, a material that can open, or which will allow sunlight to enter room.

Whatever design or material you select, you must make sure that it can be applied to the door and that doing so makes good design sense. (For example, you don't want to hang a draw drape on the front of an interior door.) The thickness and weight of the material applied to the door must be a consideration, too—a thick material may not allow the door to close, for instance. Depending on the material chosen, its weight may be beyond the capacity of door hinges. These are things that you must keep in mind when planning your installation.

I call some of my detail concepts the "no one needs to know what's behind the door" concept. Doors that are located on the flat wall of a main room, such as a

In this master bedroom, the size of the door (30 inches wide x 79 inches high) was the first consideration for the concept. Horizontal molding was installed to run the length of the wall at 81 inches off the floor (the original height of the horizontal casing). Using the original door casing as the starting point, additional 2-inch-wide molding was attached vertically to the wall in 30-inch-wide increments. Finally, grass-cloth wallpaper was applied to the wall within the 30-inch vertical spaces, including over the door and above the horizontal trim. This treatment successfully de-emphasizes the closet door.

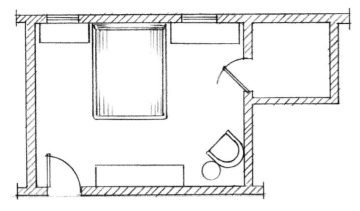

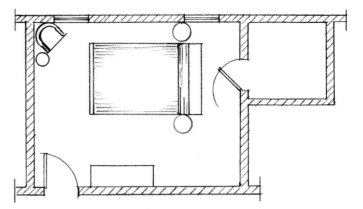

Before   After

On a personal note, I have even hidden doors in my own home. I had a closet door in one of my guest rooms that just had to go. Renovation was not an option; it never even entered my mind. The door happened to be located on the feature wall, so it was the first thing that you noticed when you entered the room.

The closet door is on the right side of the room. In my original layout a high-backed chair camouflaged the door. But, my new furniture plan called for centering the new bed in the middle of the room. The bed is a Cecil Hayes original, which I designed to be viewed from all sides. The new furniture layout placed the headboard right in front of the closet wall. To say the least, the door was an eyesore.

My solution was to panel both the door and its adjoining wall to create a seamless visual backdrop for the bed. Originally, my closet door swung into the room and was installed flush with the wall. This allowed it to become a frameless door (i.e., no molding was installed around it). To conceal the door completely, I changed the door hinges to piano hinges mounted on the inside of the door. (These are long, continuous hinges that range from 8 to 10 feet in length, will bend completely back on themselves, and use minimal space to connect the door to the wall.) Instead of traditional hardware, the closet door was installed with a touch latch (you push against the door to open and close it.) Now, despite the fact that there is a functional closet door on that wall, to the casual observer it seems that it doesn't exist. The new wall looks like one continuous wood-paneled wall.

Upon entering this client's mauve and tan bedroom, the first thing you notice is a soft silk valance paired with a shoji screen and two side drapery panels. The window treatments completely distract the viewer from the fact that there is another door on the same viewing plane. The door of the secondary master bathroom is located on the far left of the wall, but it is so completely overshadowed by the striking window treatments, that it takes the viewer a while to notice!

living room or master bedroom, are out of place in my opinion. If you are building a new home, or renovating an existing one, make certain that you relocate and/or recess doors away from the main viewing plane. If you are stuck—like I have been on several installations—with poor door placements, where it is not possible to relocate them, you can still make those offending doors "go away." All it takes is a little sleight of hand . . . and creative installation of decorative detail.

LET'S REVIEW

Walls are probably the most prominent feature of any room because of their sheer size. Therefore, wall details and designs have the ability to pull your décor all together and provide you with a one-of-a-kind look. When creating your decorative detail treatments, keep the following in mind: the style you desire, which materials would be suitable for your installation, and the method of installing your details. Among the materials that you can use to add decorative touches to your walls are:

- ⊹ Fabric
- ⊹ Metal
- ⊹ Mirror/glass
- ⊹ Molding
- ⊹ Paint
- ⊹ Stone
- ⊹ Tile
- ⊹ Wallpaper
- ⊹ Wood

The options are infinite: You can imagine more looks than you can use in a lifetime. And, if each material is that versatile on its own, just think what you can accomplish by mixing some, if not all, of them together! A cornucopia of design details awaits you.

Decorative molding is one of my favorite materials. Whether it's made of wood, stone, ceramic, or glass, I use it in almost all of my installations. Carved relief molding and/or picture framing probably appear most often as one of the key "surprise" element in my designs. That doesn't mean, however, that you should limit yourself to any one material. It's also fun to mix other media with moldings: wood moldings with stone, mirror with metal moldings, fabric with wood and paint, or wallpaper with glass. It's all good!

Wallpaper and paint are old friends. Although they are familiar to just about everybody, they can nevertheless be used to great advantage. As a decorative detail, please remember that a little goes a long way. I've used wallpaper and paint to give subtle contrast to architectural elements, even to take the place of art. Similarly, mirror/glass, plastic laminates, and metal can be used in creative ways. Whether you are creating small, jeweled accents for a paneled wall or designing a laminate treatment to surround a large plasma TV, these versatile materials can take you from A to Z with style!

Tile—whether stone, ceramic, metal, or glass—isn't just for kitchens and bathrooms anymore. I've used it to add three-dimensional impact to wall details. I've combined multiple sizes and materials in almost every installation in this book.

As you can see, decorative detailing can go from simple and sophisticated to understatedly elegant and wildly innovative. Walls accept them with open arms because the one complements the other so beautifully!

THROUGH THE EYES OF CECIL

Closet doorknobs can be replaced with touch latch mechanisms. The lack of door knob makes for better wall vs. door detailing. Bathroom doors, on the other hand, need privacy locks. So, in most cases, the knob is essential for door visibility.

4

WINDOW AND WINDOW TREATMENT DETAILS

When you think of window treatments, chances are that you will automatically think drapery; but don't let yourself get caught in the trap. By focusing entirely on soft coverings, you miss a myriad of creative options to make your windows express your unique style. Dare to think outside of the box. The end result will be well worth the effort!

In my office I used a pair of sliding shoji screens to cover my floor-to-ceiling window (with its view of the parking lot). The shoji screen frame is made of wood molding that has been painted black. The special detail, however, is the frame around the window. Here, I used black picture frame molding that is painted black but has accents of red and gold leaf. It ties into my office, which has one grass-cloth upholstered wall and three walls painted red.

THE WINDOW TREATMENTS featured in this chapter vary in style and complexity. Although I personally prefer to use more understated window treatments, there is no single formula that I follow when creating one. Each home is unique and the treatments and decorative elements are selected with this in mind.

Window treatments and trims, for our purposes, will fall into one of these categories: soft, hard, or combination. Soft treatments include fabric and fabric-based trims such as tassels and fringe. Hard treatments are based on the use of rigid material. These may include moldings and materials such as wood, Plexiglas, mirror, glass, stone, and metal. Finally, *combination treatments* are exactly what the name implies, window treatments comprised of both soft and hard elements.

Decorative window and trim details may be created using any one of the following. These are by no means all of the options:

- Drapery
- Blinds
- Cornices
- Lambrequins
- Molding
- Pelmets
- Screens
- Shades
- Valances

Each treatment may be as simple or as complex as individually desired.

SOFT TREATMENTS: DRAPERY, VALANCES, AND SHADES

Soft treatments, as you may have guessed, are fabric based. They include, among other things, drapery (both long and short), fabric valances, roller blinds, and soft shades. A combination of fabrics in the form of multiple layers, contrasting hems, pleats, linings, etc., can be used to good effect should you so desire. In addition, soft treatments are often adorned with soft trims, which include tassels, braid, fringe, and miscellaneous trims including buttons, bangles, beads, and feathers, to name just a few.

This exquisite drapery treatment features two contrasting drapery fabrics: red brocade and peach silk. The drapery has been layered for impact. Secondly, the red valances and decorative swags have been lined with peach. Then a decorative tassel fringe was allied to the edge of all the drapery, swag, and valance components. Finally, the red brocade drapery panels feature self-fabric tiebacks with tassel fringe. The peach drapery panels feature large tassel tiebacks. The overall result is opulent and impressive!

DRAPERY ✠ When I think of drapery, I always think of ladies' evening gowns. Sleek and sophisticated, or softly romantic with layers of fabric, window treatments are fabulous opportunities for decorative detailing. Window coverings such as draw drapes, swags, and valances can all accept design details. You can conceptualize the design yourself, but, unless you are an accomplished seamstress, I recommend hiring a drapery workroom to actually do the fabrication and installation.

The best decorative details for window treatments are those small touches that add interest to the whole. I am a definite believer in the axiom that less is more. You want your finished drapery treatment to be characterized by good taste and sophistication. What you don't want is for it to look like a shop window festooned with trims!

When it comes to window treatments, fabric-detailing applications can consist of fabric covering fabric, fabric lining fabric, and fabric attached to fabric, as well as any trims applied to all of the above. Trim materials range from familiar adornments including fringe, rope trim, beads, bangles, buttons, tassels, welting, and tiebacks to unusual items like feathers or even coins and medallions. You yourself can apply many of these details to existing and purchased drapery.

Hems ✣ Drapery can be hemmed in several different ways, from a basic turned hem to hems that are extra long, embellished, or made of contrasting fabrics. In drapery, hems are not limited to the bottom edge of the drape; the vertical side edges and the top edge are also candidates for decorative detailing.

Have you ever heard of puddle hemline drapery? This is where the length of the drapery is fabricated 1 to 2 feet longer than the floor level, creating a puddle effect of fabric on the floor. I think that some creative soul probably made the drapery too long to begin with, looked at the results, and thought, "What an interesting detail"—and a new look was born!

Another option is to use a different fabric for the hem of your drapery. If you like this idea, make sure that the fabric you select for the detail hem is worthy of its position. The hem should be a minimum of 3 inches in height but no more than 10 to 12 inches high. You don't want it to look like patchwork. To take the idea even further, a trim fabric of different color or design on one or both sides of the drapery (in lieu of, or in addition to, the hem) is another way to use this fabulous concept.

Pleats ✣ The interior (gusset) of a pleat is a fabulous candidate for a fabric change and is an often overlooked accent area. Whether you are talking about pleated draperies, pleated valances, pleated slipcovers, or pleated bedspreads, the inside of the pleat provides a great opportunity for adding decorative details with depth, punch, and originality. It's a small detail, but one that adds unexpected interest.

Linings ✣ Colorful linings are a popular accent choice and can be an excellent decorative detail. With drapery that is going to be clipped back to allow the lining to be exposed, an accent lining can add a new depth to your décor. Of course, drapery linings are not the only place where colorful linings can make a difference. This decorative detail can add punch to duvets, throws, and table linens.

Decorative Trims ✣ One of the simplest, and most popular, ways to detail window treatments is to add decorative trims. These trims include fringes, cording, welting, buttons, rosettes, braid, a combination of trims such as braid with tassels or cording with rosettes, and even contrasting fabric hems. As a general rule, decorative trims are purchased ready-made and applied to the drapery. You can let your imagination soar when it comes to decorative trims, but always keep the drapery

The valance on this window treatment features a contrasting header that is a bit wider than the quite narrow 1-inch pleated contrasting hem. Three contrasting bows round out the look.

The contrast in these drapery linings comes not from the color but from the fabric selection. The front of the drapery features a stripe in soft cream and green. The reverse, with its plaid pattern, also matches the cream-and-green color scheme. Design and photo © Waverly

function firmly in mind. There's no right or wrong when it comes to drapery trims, but things like tassels on the hem of drapery can be sucked away by the vacuum cleaner. Just a little consumer note!

Both large- and small-scale window treatments can afford to be adorned with trims. As you detail, however, make sure the detail does not become a distraction. The use of trims on large panels of fabric is a great look when it accessorizes the window cover. But, laying too many trims is the fashion equivalent of layering on too much jewelry.

Tiebacks ✠ Drapery tiebacks offer yet another opportunity to introduce an accent fabric or trim into the décor. Tiebacks hold the drapery panels in place when you pull them to the sides of the window with some sort of decorative bracket or holder—hence the name "tieback." These decorative brackets can be made of metal, plastic, wood, or stone. I've even made unusual brackets out of remnants of carved screens (see page 156 for an example).

Tiebacks can be also be made from soft trims. Large tassels are the most popular option, probably because they are so readily available for purchase. It's also common for tiebacks to be made of fabric. These can be as simple as a matching fabric plait or as flamboyant as a contrasting fabric adorned with trims. Whether you opt for coordinating or contrasting tiebacks, the choice is yours.

Tiebacks are one of those areas where you can put your hands to work and make your own. You can use various materials including large bows, yarns, rope, fabric, jewelry, chain, shells, raffia, beads, pearls, ceramic tile, and silk flowers, among other things. The possibilities are only limited by your imagination! Recently, I installed a job using a large tieback that featured an oval wood plaque with a carved relief of a man's head and black silk yarns extending from the bottom. It was one of the most unusual applications that I've used.

VALANCES ✠ A valance is a type of horizontal treatment used to frame a window and hide the curtain rods. Like its cousin, the cornice, it sits at the top of the window. Unlike a cornice, which has a base made of wood materials, a valance is made exclusively of soft, flowing fabrics. Valance fabrics can be shirred, pleated, gathered, or draped, and their hems can be straight or shaped (points, scallops, etc.) and adorned with trims (like braiding, tassels, or fringe). The valance can match, complement, or contrast with the drapery fabric. The fluid form of the valance offers another opportunity to introduce decorative detailing through the use of linings and trims.

Note the deep gold bullion fringe that finishes the elegant drapery/valance treatment. Large tieback tassels in matching gold hold back the drapery panels.

THROUGH THE
EYES OF CECIL

Personally, I am an earring girl. I always select them to add the final accent to my attire, and the right pair—either large or small—can really finish off the look in style. That's why earrings are always the final selection I make when I am "putting on the Ritz" to step out. It's all about adding the finishing touches. That's probably why I call tiebacks the "earrings" of window dressing. They add personality and accent details to any interior window covering, and can really finish off the look with style. Small or large, simple or extravagant, tiebacks are the quintessential decorative detail for any interior.

Most people think of large drapery tassels when they think tieback, but in this case, the fabric tieback on this layered window treatment actually matches its lining fabric and provides good contrast to the top layer of the treatment. It is an unusual oversized application.

Paisley is always rich and elegant, and this valance is no exception. The cream lining, cord trim, and covered buttons contrast nicely against the pleated paisley fabric. Installed over a rattan blind in the same shades of cream and black and brown it makes for an unforgettable window treatment. Design (pattern 5057) © Butterick

This pleated cornice treatment combines a striped fabric with a Moroccan-inspired print and beaded trimmings. It's an unusual application, which combines a fabric valance over an upholstered cornice with striking results. Design (pattern 5057) © Butterick

SHADES AND BLINDS ✠ Fabric shades are available in many styles, from the frothy (Austrian) to the austere (Roman), and just about all of us have run into the old roller blind at some point in our lives. Shades make excellent substitutes for full-fledged drapery treatments and can be homemade, custom made, or purchased. Despite their less exalted status, however, shades can just as easily benefit from decorative detail concepts as drapery does.

THROUGH THE EYES OF CECIL

In my first book, *9 Steps to Beautiful Living*, I explained how windows and walls are natural partners. For this reason, window and wall concepts should be planned together to create a finish detail.

What do you get when you combine a Roman shade with a valance? This beautiful window treatment, which combines a striped fabric in shades of tan, green, gold, and violet, dressed with silk cord and finished with a single soft tassel. It's very chic, and understatedly elegant. Design (pattern 5059) © Butterick

THROUGH THE EYES OF CECIL

For me, shoji screens don't always mean that a room has an Asian-inspired décor, but rather that it would benefit from a straight-line, architectural window treatment.

HARD TREATMENTS: SCREENS, MOLDING, AND CORNICES

Hard treatments, as I define them, use wood or other rigid materials as the basis for the design. These treatments may include screens, molding, wood cornices, and blinds (both vertical and Venetian), lambrequins, and pelmets. Sometimes the treatment takes its inspiration from Oriental design. Other times it takes the "less is more" approach and relies on the application of simple molding to frame a window. Occasionally, we go completely over the top with European-inspired lambrequins and pelmets. Whatever form it takes, hard window treatments and trims make for unusual decorative detailing.

SHOJI SCREENS ⊕ The shoji screen is a window covering that originated in Japan. The screen itself is usually comprised of a pair (or more) of wood-framed, sectioned panels, each section of which is filled with rice paper or sheer fabric. Traditionally the panels are painted black. Shoji screens have many uses—as doors, window coverings, and stationary screens, to name just a few. Generally, shoji screens are sliding panels, which run on both an upper and a lower track.

Creating a shoji screen treatment on a grand scale, this two-story great room combines decorative molding with columns, detail elements, and Hunter Douglas' Duet window shades. The upper bank of windows is framed by large-scale moldings and screened by the shades to softly filter the light.

The wooden frame on the shoji screen is where molding can add exceptional detailing to your look. For example, if your look is traditional, use molding with a profile to frame out your screen. On the other hand, if you go for a more contemporary look, keep the molding flat. A lightweight, semi-opaque material is stretched tight and applied to the back of each panel, using nails, staples, or glue. The semi-opaque material allows light to flow through, while providing privacy.

Shoji screens are wonderful window coverings to use in detail concepts that are simple and serene. I've used shoji screens in many installations. I select them for varying reasons, but I tend to use them in contemporary spaces or when I want to create a more informal interior décor. I also tend to use them when I want the emphasis to remain on the architectural elements rather than decorative adornment.

In this master bedroom, the installation just creates the illusion of a shoji screen. Using Japanese ash (which is what the window blind is made of), I framed out the windows and continued that framing along with the bed wall. The stationary windows at the top have been framed out and covered with a woven lattice of Japanese ash. The resulting treatment is simple, stylish, and Asian influenced.

MOLDING-BASED WINDOW TREATMENTS ✤ Molding has great applications for window trimming and detailing. In fact, many of us are already accustomed to seeing molding used to frame a window (in which case it is called the window casing). The look is not difficult to achieve. Often, people are afraid applied molding may be too stark in their space. This has not been the case in my experience, but if you are concerned about using this type of treatment, remember one thing: You can always add additional layers to soften or embellish the look.

You may be faced with an unusual window location, which needs some adornment. In this client's home, I chose a simple molding to frame out a ceiling-height window between two rooms. Because the furniture plan called for an entertainment unit to be located directly below this window, I used the furniture to balance the window. The stain color makes the window and wall unit become one.

WOODEN CORNICES: *The Unexpected Application* ✠ Normally cornices are covered with fabric, or painted. But, a stained wooden cornice can be a stunning, sophisticated design detail in any room. Wooden cornices are particularly dramatic with modern and contemporary décor.

In lieu of a standard window treatment, I installed a large wooden cornice. The cornice acts as both window trim and a wall detail.

COMBINATION TREATMENTS

Combination treatments are exactly what the name implies—window treatments comprised of both soft and hard elements. They may be found in many forms, but the most common are cornices and pelmets. Occasionally I have even combined architectural elements with fabric-based ones with good effect.

CORNICES ✤ A horizontal treatment used to frame a window and hide the curtain rods, a cornice sits at the top of the window. It is loosely defined as a decorative horizontal band of straight or shaped wood that can be covered with decorative elements such as wallpaper, paint, or fabric.

Because the cornice back is made of wood, you can add fabrics, papers, and even decorative moldings by gluing, stapling, or nailing them directly to the backing board. If you add molding to the cornice, I recommend that you first apply the decorative covering to the cornice, before you add the finish molding. And be sure to paint or stain the molding before adding it to the cornice.

Cornices always have a return on each end (like a box) to cover the drapery hardware, and you will need to make two mitered cuts and joins at each end of the cornice. You need to know what window treatment you plan to use before you begin fabrication of the cornice, because the depth of the window covering directly affects the depth of the window cornice. Two things to remember: (1) To determine the necessary depth of the cornice, measure the depth of the proposed window covering and add a minimum of 1 inch to get your required depth; (2) when using a window covering that pulls up (e.g., Roman shade), make sure that you get the stack measurements of the shade from the work room, and again add at least 1 inch. Further application of crown molding (or any other molding) can be used to give a stately looking treatment to your cornice.

This deep-pink upholstered cornice features four mirrored heart appliqués trimmed out with hot pink fur. It may not be to everyone's taste, but there is no doubt that it makes for an eye-catching decorative detail.

PELMETS ✠ Technically, a pelmet is also defined as a piece of straight or shaped wood that can be covered with decorative elements such as wallpaper, paint, or fabric. In order to distinguish it from its sibling the cornice, however, I define a pelmet as a piece of straight or shaped wood that is used in conjunction with soft drapery materials. The wood pelmet stands alone as an integral part of the composition.

Molding can be used to create a fabulous pelmet (or cornice) for any window! Any carved or profile molding will do, but personally I think that large dental molding is especially nice in this application. It makes an ordinary window something special to behold. To create a pelmet like that, you could use either a single- or a double-width of molding. If you use a double-width, try gluing them top-to-top for added emphasis. Then, install a large square of wood at each end of the molding to serve as finials, and apply a bracket to each end of the treatment so that it can be installed on the wall. Finally, staple your fabric to the back side of the molding, manipulating the fabric to obtain the desired look: panels, swags, or a combination of both. The result: a stationary window treatment that is something out of the ordinary

In this window treatment, a simple pelmet made of wood molding is further embellished with decorative gilding.

Some decorative window treatments are designed for effect not function. Such is the case with this dining room window treatment. The stationary drapery hangs from a series of finials, symmetrically placed inside the deep-set arch of the window.

One of the key components of this innovative window treatment is the curtain rod. Not so unusually, the drapery is hung over a contrasting Roman shade within the window casing, but it is the rod treatment that lifts this window treatment out of the ordinary. It puts a new spin on the purely functional and makes a definite statement.

ADDING OOMPH WITH PURCHASED ACCESSORIES ✛ There are a lot of decorative window treatment options that you can buy ready-made in retail stores and on the Web. The home decorator will find literally hundreds to choose from in materials ranging from glass to metal to wood. There's nothing wrong with using purchased accessories to create your decorative details if you so desire. In fact, it can be a fast and inexpensive way to detail.

LET'S REVIEW

When you think of window treatments, chances are that you will automatically think of drapery or soft window coverings. While these are great options, there are many other creative applications for window treatments. Soft window coverings such as drapery, valances, and shades are readily familiar to most homeowners. Decorative treatments based on the use of wood, wood moldings, and other rigid materials, on the other hand, may be something entirely new to the average consumer. There are also combination treatments which, as the name implies, are created from a combination of soft and hard window treatments and trims.

Soft treatments are based on the manipulation of fabric and usually involve the application of purchased trims or other detail elements to create impact. Some options employ contrast: layering contrasting fabrics; applying contrasting headers, hems, or borders; fabricating draperies with contrasting linings; and applying contrasting purchased trims.

Treatments based on wood, such as shoji screens and trim details, are more architectural in nature and will require the assistance of a skilled woodworker. Shoji screens, while listed under hard trims in this chapter, are actually a combination of hard and soft elements. Architecturally based trims tend to be more understated and are perfect when you wish to keep the emphasis on the architecture of a space and not on decorative ornamentation.

Occasionally you can create a window treatment, that relies heavily on purchased accessories for effect. I like to use unusual items to provide the mechanics for hanging drapery. Finials, doorknobs, architectural salvage such as corbels and pelmets, unique pieces of drapery hardware, etc. can all be used to good effect.

Window trims and treatments are another area in the home where you can really put your imagination to work. If you come up with a concept, you like it, and you think it will look good, go on and give it a try. From personal experience I have found that you may have to fine-tune the concept a bit, but in the end you will end up with one-of-a-kind treatment that reflects the true spirit of the home.

THROUGH THE EYES OF CECIL

I love a room with a view. When the view is breathtaking, I use minimal window treatments. When the view is not so wonderful, I allow the window treatment to become my view.

ARCHITECTURAL DETAILS

Have you ever seen something and thought that with just a little work it could be transformed into something even better? That's the entire concept behind architectural detailing. It's all about looking for architectural elements in your home that you can make into detail wonders. When I look at a space for the first—or even second—time, I try to find an architectural element that catches my eye. This type of element is already prominent and, with just a little special detailing, it can become something extraordinary.

Take a look at the decorative niche in this soffit area above another client's bar. Lighting has been installed both within the niche and beneath the soffit. In the niche, it serves to highlight my client's sculptures. Recessed hi-hat fixtures serve to direct ambient lighting into the bar area. The decorative faux paint band at the base of the soffit helps to further define the area.

ARCHITECTURAL DETAILING IS about creating decorative detailing concepts that make use of the architectural elements of a space. These elements fall into two categories: structural and nonstructural. Structural elements cannot be removed without compromising the structural integrity of the space. Nonstructural elements, on the other hand, have been added purely for aesthetics. They have no mechanical or structural purpose, and can be added, modified, or even removed without dire consequences. Throughout my career, I've worked with both elements to customize my clients' homes.

Here are some of the most common structural and nonstructural architectural elements that can lay the foundation for your decorative detailing:

- Columns
- Doors and windows (both interior and exterior)
- Doorways and pass-throughs
- Fireplaces
- Niches
- Soffits
- Staircases and steps

Existing architectural elements can be *adorned* with a myriad of materials including wood, stone, tile, glass, mirror, fabric, and metal. We can also *create* architectural elements out of these same materials. Both methods have the same goal: to enhance the space.

A soffit should define its setting. When design-

ing detail treatments for soffits, my thoughts

are always directed toward what is below the

soffit. Narrow soffit depth is a great definer for

consoles, upper kitchen cabinets, vanities, and

headboard walls. Deep soffit depth makes a

great definer for bar areas, dining rooms, or any

area that is separated from a furniture grouping

and large enough to define its own space.

In this chapter, I suggest some architectural areas that may benefit from the application of decorative detailing. Of course, once you begin to look around for yourself, I'm confident that you can find many more opportunities for your own brand of creativity.

STRUCTURAL INSTALLATIONS

Just for the record, structural elements are those that are necessary for the structural integrity of the space. These elements may include columns, doors, windows, staircases, fireplaces, and soffits. The key thing to keep in mind about structural elements is that they cannot be removed without adverse consequences. Columns may be either structural or nonstructural, but in this chapter we'll only discuss structural columns. If you are not absolutely certain whether the column you want to move is structural or not, bring in an experienced professional who can tell you with certainty.

SOFFITS ☦ Many homes have areas with soffits (loosely defined as the underside of any architectural element such as an arch, beam, lintel, or cornice). These are generally used to conceal mechanical items—for example, in condos they often conceal air-conditioning and heating ductwork—or to provide for a change in ceiling height and/or give additional dimension to walls.

Most often they are made of building material, such as drywall. The drop soffits that accent any small space are a great place for decorative detailing and should not be ignored.

In this modern dining room, the soffit area runs around the entire perimeter of the rectangular room, leaving space for decorative detail in the form of an oval tray ceiling at the center. The soffit houses both concealed cove lighting and recessed hi-hat fixtures. The large oval chandelier echoes the form of the soffit.

COLUMNS ✛ Architecturally speaking, structural columns cannot be removed without causing serious structural issues in your design space. Therefore, columns are one of those structural elements that you will have to work with or work around. I'm sure that some of you have already had to deal with a structural column located somewhere you really didn't want it. I call this "in your face" decorating. (Translation: It's in your way, and you can't do a thing about it.) Well, you're not alone. As you'll see in the following installations, there are many creative ways to turn these clunky obstacles into eye-popping design details.

Sometimes an addition (or extension) to an existing house will require the use of support columns. In this case, you do have the option of removing the structural column—you can spend thousands of dollars to have it taken out and replaced with steel beams. Before you choose that road, however, why not take the time to think about how you can turn this into an architectural detail? It'll be much easier on your pocketbook, and much more rewarding!

THROUGH THE EYES OF CECIL

There are three fundamental concepts to consider when enhancing structural columns:

- ✛ Create "partners" such as room dividers, niches, art walls, or additional columns.

- ✛ Build walls or room dividers to conceal.

- ✛ Enlarge size to display small paintings.

Note: A structural column can be anywhere from 4 inches x 4 inches, up to 12 inches x 12 inches.

This penthouse unit in a high-rise condominium had a gorgeous ocean view; it was truly breathtaking. The open living space offered many design possibilities, but when I saw the large structural column in the middle of the open space, it temporarily took the wind out of my sails.

Working around it was certainly a possibility, but I found myself thinking, "Why?" After all, the column was doing what it was designed to do. But, if I didn't work around it, what would I do with it? Then I remembered one of my maxims: No single unit should stand alone. Eureka! There was my solution.

I had my contractor build another column (the same size) 4 feet away and parallel to the existing one. A bridge was installed at the top of the two columns to connect them and to house additional lighting. Finally, a stainless bracket was added, which was designed to support the large pieces of art that we had designated to hang between the columns. When completed, the two-column structure neatly divided the living room from the dining room and provided display spaces for two pieces of art from the client's collection, one on each side of the structure.

On this project, I created a room divider that houses both mechanical elements and encases structural columns. It wasn't my original concept, but the end result was well worth the sacrifices we had to make to get there.

The home in question was built on a grand scale, which was embodied in the 14-foot ceilings in the living and family rooms, and the kitchen. The main rooms were originally divided by one wall with two entrances. One entrance led from the living room to the family room. The second led from the kitchen to the dining room. The original design concept was to simply enlarge the entrance space between the living and family rooms, but it had to be abandoned because there was a structural column located in the wall at precisely the point where we wanted to enlarge the opening.

I went back to the drawing board and ultimately developed a new concept that turned out to be stunning and more than compensated us for having to sacrifice the original plan. A display unit of half-round columns covered with textured stone rises to the ceiling. Each column area houses several decorative niches, which have been backed with mirror. Eight feet above the floor, a drywall soffit connects the columns and houses lighting as well as the air-conditioning duct and vent. The new dividing wall is the perfect display area for the clients' collection of bronze sculptures.

One of my most recent support-column challenges arose in this Miami home purchased by one of my clients. The original space did not match his personality and his sense of style—slick contemporary. We intended to follow the less-is-more approach by removing a pair of existing colonial columns and leaving the space completely open. During demolition, however, we discovered that one of those columns was actually structural and would have to stay. Since we had to keep one column, we decided to keep them both, but to recreate them in a way that was much more in keeping with the owner's aesthetic sensibilities. Voilà—new columns that are high-tech in nature, composed of lacquer wood with stainless steel accents.

Most of the columns in this room are made of glass. And when I say "made," I truly mean it. We combined multiple layers of vertically stacked ¾-inch, chiseled-edge glass to create the glass surface of the stem of each column. When you combine multiple pieces of glass this thick, you create the impression of glass in motion. I love that the layers of glass change in color from clear to green or aqua based on the combination. I am always in awe of the way glass can change its character.

STAIRCASES AND STEPS

Believe it or not, staircases are another architectural element where you can use the structure to enhance your personal design objectives. It can be as easy as detailing the stair risers (or even the treads!) or as involved as demolishing and reconstructing the entire staircase as a creative detail in and of itself. Big or small, making changes to stairs can result in a stunning design impact.

OPPOSITE ✤ A more modern trend calls for the wooden banister railing to give way to a detail statement in stainless steel and glass, which lets light permeate all layers of the home and contributes to the open, airy feel of the space. In this instance, the staircase, with its maple treads, was cantilevered over the formal living room. This striking treatment allows the homeowners to carry their décor throughout both levels without visual distraction.

SUPPORTING THE STAIR ✤ Making an actual structural change is at least as challenging as camouflaging a structural eyesore. The relocation and redesign of a staircase presents both a visual and a structural challenge. You have to think about the look and the functionality of the stairs at *both* ends of the staircase, both the upstairs and the downstairs spaces. Be prepared to be flexible in the process. Sometimes a design looks good on paper, but during construction, many variables can lead you to discover an entirely different approach.

To highlight the change in elevation between the dining and living areas of this client's home, I used three different flooring materials in the design. All are neutral in color, so they work well together visually, but because each has a unique texture, it is immediately apparent that there is a change in elevation between the rooms.

PLAYING UP CHANGES IN ELEVATION ✣ When I began my career, one of the hot design trends was the "change in elevation." Architects of the period delighted in creating sunken living rooms (or raised dining areas). In fact, this trend is still common in homes with large open areas. Like my contemporaries, I used to downplay the variations in elevation within a room so as not to distract from the overall impact of my décor. But that was before a conversation with one of my clients. "Cecil," she said, "people love the décor. I am getting so many compliments. But, I'm having a real problem here, too. My guests are so caught up in looking around my beautiful home, that I have had several people fall over the step into the dining area. Can you recommend something?"

Well, as you can imagine, that really made me think. Obviously, I wanted my clients and their guests to enjoy the interior that I had created for them, but I didn't want them to break their necks doing it! That was the moment I decided to begin playing up changes in elevation. My preferred method for accomplishing this is to add an accent material (i.e., a change of flooring material) or a design detail to the tread of the step that contrasts with the lower floor covering so that the eye instantly recognizes the change.

Another often-overlooked area for decorative detailing is the stair riser (the back, vertical part of the stair which you see when looking up the staircase), which is usually painted an uninspiring neutral. Why not jazz this area up with tile detailing or creative painting? It would guarantee that your staircase will be noticed.

THROUGH THE EYES OF CECIL

I tend to use natural materials and/or neutral colors when I select flooring because I find that it creates the most complementary background for the room's décor. With a neutral floor color, even a somewhat subtle color change in the riser(s) of the stair(s) will be easy to see. Safety, I have found, can be beautiful!

By varying the materials and introducing a strong color on the riser, in contrast to the neutral color of the flooring, I created a strong delineation between the two floor levels.

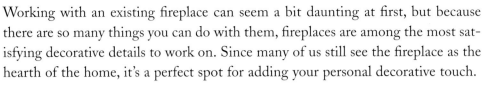

Many parts of a fireplace can accept special

design detailing. For me, however, the mantel

is my focal detail because it is the deepest

part of the fireplace, and it's at eye level, the

position most worthy of attention.

FIREPLACES

Working with an existing fireplace can seem a bit daunting at first, but because there are so many things you can do with them, fireplaces are among the most satisfying decorative details to work on. Since many of us still see the fireplace as the hearth of the home, it's a perfect spot for adding your personal decorative touch.

In one of my most recent installations, the 18-foot-high fireplace in a living room is faced in various sized rectangles of coral stone, which is rough in texture. A large triangular-shaped stainless steel mantel brings sleek, smooth sophistication to the textured wall. A custom-manufactured fire screen of sandblasted glass and stainless steel add to the contemporary design detail.

BELOW ✤ In this cozy living room, the tone of the décor was established with the combination of wooden ceiling, stone floor, and textured stone fascia on the fireplace. The room was originally intended for an informal décor, but new owners preferred a more formal space. They requested that I keep the wood ceiling and stone coverings, but give it a sense of stately presence. I added the mantel and decorative fireplace surround—made of cherrywood with a motif of relief profiles carved into both the mantel and surround—which created a formal setting.

ABOVE ✤ The marble-covered fireplace wall is 18 feet tall. For visual interest I designed a two-tier custom stainless steel mantel and soffit treatment, a design inspired by my client's love of candlelight.

The first time I met my client at his home, I noticed that he'd placed lighted candles on various tables all around the living room. My imagination was fired! The client enjoys a contemporary design aesthetic, and that brought stainless steel immediately to mind. I knew he enjoyed the scent and glow of candles, which made me think in terms of reflected surfaces. I began to think about a more creative way to present those flickering candles, and that, in turn, led me to the idea of a metal mantel with cutout openings to reveal the glow and aroma of the candles. I wanted to replicate the hearth blaze with tiny flames above it. A great idea (if I say so myself) ignited by the light of a candle. The result: the large flames in the fireplace are reflected in, and complemented by, the small flames in the metal above. I couldn't resist it, and my client loved it.

In creating the custom fireplace treatment for this eclectic Florida home, I installed 18-inch x 18-inch gold metal tile with etched swirl lines around the face of the fire box. The mantel and uprights are custom carved wood with a high-gloss, white lacquer finish. The addition of the gold tile creates a very special decorative detail, and is one which may not have been an obvious choice given the style of décor.

MOLDING FOR INTERIOR AND EXTERIOR DOORS

There are many styles and sizes of standard molding, a design element familiar to most people because it is so often used to frame doorways. Typically, the molding takes the form of the door case (all the joinery work that frames or surrounds a door), all of which are necessary to support the door function. Of course, when there is no door installed in the opening, the molding becomes an optional design element.

Decorative molding, in addition to adorning a flat door, can also be used to smooth the transition between one space and another. In tract-built homes, the simple archway is often the predominant transition between rooms. However, if your decorating scheme is vibrant in one room and more subdued in the next, how do you transition gracefully? The answer may lie with decorative moldings and casings.

INTERIOR DOORS AND OPENINGS ⊹ Interior doors and openings (such as archways) are excellent places to use decorative molding, both flat and profile. I have used moldings for these purposes throughout my career. I find it works equally well for traditional and contemporary interior applications, as long as you keep in mind the period for which you are designing. Flat moldings can be made to work for all types of interiors; profile moldings should be used with more caution. The more elaborate the molding, the more traditional the design application.

In the case of this bright gold door, the décor of the adjoining room is not meant to be a secret. The large center panel of the door is an etched glass design, which is part clear and part opaque. The clear glass reveals a wine room that houses over five hundred bottles of fine wine. (Did I mention my client is a professionally trained chef and wine connoisseur?)

One client's home is a mix of antiques and eclectic furnishings and accessories, characterized by a series of archways leading from one space to another. In one area of the home, we had a display/entertainment cabinet, which was located adjacent to an arched entry. We replicated that arched molding on the wall unit and the doorway.

OPPOSITE ✛ Wood paneling in this foyer also serves to "square up" the entrance into the family room. The unusual depth (18 inches vs. the usual 5 inches) of the doorway opening gives additional visual strength to the design.

THROUGH THE EYES OF CECIL

Interior doorways don't all have to look the same. As long as you are careful not to have too many different treatments on the same viewing plane, there is no rule that says everything has to match exactly. One of the easiest ways to obtain distinction is by adding or modifying moldings (and door casings) to impart different looks to the individual entrances.

This client loves contemporary style. As a result, he requested that the door to his bedroom make a statement that reflected his modern design aesthetic. I added contemporary character and mixed-media appeal to the doors with a combination of raised metal panels and flat wood molding. This concept (or something quite similar) could easily be put to work in your own home.

THROUGH THE EYES OF CECIL

The front entrance is the most important door of the home for style detail. The front door sets the design tone for both the exterior and interior of the home. I always make them special!

EXTERIOR DOORS ✣ Exterior doors and openings are also perfect places to use decorative molding. As details, they can bring excitement to those places we see every day. At the same time, decorative detailing can make it perfectly clear that this is no ordinary, cookie-cutter-variety home!

The framing of my front door (and windows) started with a great find: a pair of antique doors. Ornate and heavy in appearance, the doors overwhelmed the original entry of my home, both structurally and aesthetically. But I had to have those doors! So, instead of hiring a contractor and removing the existing doorframe, we refaced the existing paint-grade door and window molding with teak. This provided the structural strength needed to hang the doors, and gave the home and entrance the visual strength to compete with them. The decorative element on the molding, supplied by the half-round wooden balls, was inspired by the design on the doors themselves.

NONSTRUCTURAL INSTALLATIONS

Most homes these days include only the most basic, essential architectural details—those necessary for structural reasons. Purely decorative elements, which would add interest from a design standpoint, are not even considered. No bump-outs, soffits, or niches. These homes/interior spaces are simply square or rectangular boxes defined as rooms. They are perfectly adequate functioning spaces, even if somewhat uninspiring. By adding creative detailing, however, you not only personalize your space, you add excitement.

SOFFITS ✧ Soffits are some of the easiest nonstructural additions that you can make to a home. They are basically drywall boxes, which are usually installed at ceiling height in any given room or space. However, that doesn't mean that you are limited to a ceiling installation—soffits can be installed vertically or horizontally at any height. Generally, they are used to conceal light fixtures or heat and air-conditioning ductwork, but they can also be added for pure aesthetic appeal and adorned with fabulous results.

In one client's small powder bath, the builder added a large arch with a drywall soffit to define the sink area. My design called for a traditional console vanity and a crystal vessel sink, but the drywall arch overshadowed out the light appearance of these fixtures and caused the room to appear unbalanced. To counteract that, I rebalanced the room through my choice of decorative detail. The combination of a curved white tile (called pillow talk), and a small engraved metal tile, used as an insert, lifted the bathroom to new heights. The tile added softness, and also movement to the soffit.

DECORATIVE COLUMNS FOR DRAMA AND
ADDED DETAILING ✣ Decorative columns, an architectural element that
I frequently use in my design concepts, are generally inspired by the overall design
aesthetic of the project. These columns are not for structural support, but rather
for purposes of impact and drama. Towering columns are wonderful details, and
they are more dramatic than beautiful furniture, accessories, and art combined.

If you're looking for a stunning way to introduce a space,
it doesn't get better than the grandeur of these columns
(one of which is shown here.) Inspired by Moroccan
architecture, they were fabricated in my shop and
installed on-site to provide dramatic detailing between the
two main living spaces in this home. The two beautiful
Japanese ash columns gently complement the existing
wood trim in both the living and dining rooms. They were
installed within a custom-designed drywall soffit, which
gently embraces them and captures the graceful lines of
the carved wood. The base is made of stainless steel, and
ties into the silver, metal, and ash wood décor. Both

Using Multiple Materials When Designing Decorative Columns ✠ Decorative detailing, as you know, is all about adding interesting touches to an interior. Various materials can be used to add architectural interest, running the gamut from hard to soft, from metal to glass. There is no hard-and-fast rule that says that you cannot use multiple materials or coordinating designs within a single installation. I love to mix things up by juxtaposing multiple materials and styles within my installations. It's fun, funky, and totally unexpected!

THROUGH THE EYES OF CECIL

I visualize columns in my interior space as a detail. I use them to divide a space, to define a space, even to give architectural strength to an existing room. To me, the decorative column is a quintessential decorative detail.

These columns were designed to "light up" the space—quite literally! The grand teak columns are topped by stainless steel sconces, and the light adds unlooked-for interest and detail to the columns and imparts a glow to the ceiling.

USING EXOTIC MATERIALS TO CREATE DARING

DECORATIVE DETAILS ✣ There are design concepts that I refer to as details purely because of the unusual material that I used. Texture, color, and type of material can transform an ordinary-looking room into a custom-designed space. These materials can be expensive, but the payoff can be well worth it. By using exotic coverings and materials, you can transform an everyday look into a real looker.

This should have been a simple installation. After all, I was installing two very simple, albeit large, wooden columns at the entrance to the family and living room areas. These 18-inch-square and 12-feet-high columns were nothing to write home about, until you actually saw the exotic material from which they were made: zebrawood.

Zebrawood is a fabulous design material. This exotic wood has two colors (light and dark) in its vertical grain, hence the name "zebrawood." When properly used, this wood is sheer visual dynamite! But, it was a bit overwhelming in this space, where the only things you saw were two large columns in the middle of an otherwise undecorated space, so I understood why my clients had anxiety about them.

I wanted to save the zebrawood (which I knew, based on the overall design, was right for the space). I explained to the clients that it was a bit early to judge how the room would look when it was finished, and reminded them about the other decorative elements that would go in the room, such as the neutral-colored fabrics, walls, and window coverings. I'd selected zebrawood because the colors in the grain accented the colors of the other decorative elements my clients had already chosen. It was the zebrawood, I assured them, and not the column itself, which would give the space that wonderful designer detail. They were soothed, although slightly dubious, and agreed to move forward with the design. Three weeks later, once the home was finished and the furniture and decorative accents were completely installed, the look was, and *is*, fantastic. Ask my clients today, and they will tell you that they absolutely love it! (See page 172 for detailed working drawing of this entertainment unit.)

STRUCTURAL ART NICHES

I like adding art and display niches to the homes that I design. It's a little thing, but an art niche adds a sense of drama when properly placed. It's a great way to show off favorite art pieces, such as sculptures and paintings, within a single area.

PLAYING UP A NICHE ✤ There are many creative ways that you can play up this already outstanding feature. Personally, my favorite technique is to contrast the finish inside the niche with that of the outside wall. The contrast can be subtle, or it can be dramatic.

Many times a niche detail can be developed into something unexpected. In my clients' dining room, the original plan called for two large niches to house sculpture and artwork. But I realized those niches would also be the perfect spaces to house cabinets that didn't take up floor space. With that in mind, I created two special furniture pieces—a wine storage niche made of wood, metal, and faux stone (for decorative detail), and directly across from the wine storage niche, I created a wooden china cabinet.

THROUGH THE EYES OF CECIL

In pondering jobs requiring new construction or minimal renovation, I see niches at the end of hallways. I see recesses on large walls. And I see three-dimensional art and paintings located in these niches. I use the private enclosure area of a niche to make reasonably priced items priceless!

Of course, you don't have to limit yourself to paint, either. Niches are all about making the viewer notice the art and accessories. I also advocate installing light fixtures in art niches. A small round puck light or spotlight really wakes the niche up after dark and shows your art to its best advantage.

Display niches have a way of making an inexpensive item appear expensive. It's like a confidence trick for your décor. The very act of placing a piece of art or sculpture into an art niche does something to the viewer's perception. First, it draws their attention. Then, it adds prominence and importance to the object so elevated. Finally, it confers distinction. You can always find an item to place within a niche, be it a painting, a vase, a vessel, or a sculpture.

Creating a nonstructural wall niche is not difficult. Niches do not require knocking out a wall and, in fact, are usually built in front of an existing wall. Standard depth for a niche is 4- to 6-inches deep for a framed painting, or 12- to 18-inches deep for a sculpture or three-dimensional piece of art. I usually recommend that the base of the niche be situated no less than 24 inches above the finished floor.

The inside of the art niche in this home has been painted in subtle contrast to the remainder of the wall, a treatment that serves to subtly emphasize the art. The location/size of an art niche can always be balanced by the addition of art and furniture.

When you want to add even more emphasis to your art collection, I recommend using a contrasting paint color on the inside of the niche. This is one way to make the art displayed "pop" even more!

Art niches are great additions for the dead end of a wall, like those I created for my guest suite. My home features a split bedroom plan, which results in two hallways that lead to the guest bedrooms. At the dead end of this hallway, the art niche provides added depth and interest.

THROUGH THE EYES OF CECIL

The story of the transformation of this boxy room is required reading for anyone who wants to add the look of structural detailing to a home without the mess of construction. All the features pictured here were fabricated at the mill shop and then installed on site.

This great room was one big box of a room—26 feet long x 16 feet wide x 18 feet high. The space was screaming for some personality. I began on the feature/sofa wall, adding two wooden display columns that span floor to ceiling and which gave much-needed dimension to the flat wall. We built a soffit over the sofa area to lower the ceiling and to create a more human scale, and added two smaller wooden columns to introduce the large archway.

The fixed windows were positioned about 8 feet above the floor and joined by glass doors below. The view of the pool area and golf course was too magnificent to cover, so I framed the windows using wood and glass panels.

TRANSFORMING BOXY SPACES

As I've said before, homes built today tend to have minimal architectural detailing. Most rooms are basically plain boxes with nothing to engage one's interest. But it doesn't always have to stay that way. With careful planning you can rework your "box" and transform it into something entirely different.

LET'S REVIEW

Architectural elements can be the perfect starting point for your decorative detail concepts. In fact, I always look to the architectural elements when I am developing my interior designs. I try to find elements that catch my eye and incorporate them into the decorative treatment. Because they are already prominent, with just a little special detailing, you can create something extraordinary.

When working with architectural elements, you should know that there are two types: structural and nonstructural. Structural elements *cannot* be removed without seriously damaging the building. Nonstructural elements, on the other hand, can be subtracted without fear because they are purely decorative. It is absolutely vital that you understand the difference between the two and how to determine which is which *before* your begin working on your home project. (Note: If you are ever in doubt, have it evaluated by a competent professional.)

Some of the elements that can benefit from decorative detailing include soffits, columns, staircases and steps, fireplaces, doors and doorways, windows, and niches, both structural and nonstructural. Others, especially fireplaces, staircases, and support columns, are purely structural and should be modified with care.

Already-existing elements can be adorned with a myriad of materials among which are wood, metal, glass, tile, mirror, paint, paper, and fabric-based materials. There is nothing that says that you cannot dress up a soffit with paint, tile, or even track lighting should you so desire. Additionally, you could reface the stair treads or select contrasting material to highlight a change of elevation. And, when you're working with structural elements, there is nothing in the Decorator's Handbook that says you can't hire a professional contractor, as I have done with some of my staircase installations.

Because much of today's new construction lacks significant architectural detailing, one of the easiest ways to add impact to a new home can be to install your own architectural elements. These run the gamut from wood molding to decorative soffits to faux columns and beyond. The goal here is to create character. Since the elements don't have to perform a structural function, you can allow your imagination full rein when creating these details. Whether structural or nonstructural, as long as you keep your overall design aesthetic firmly in mind, you can create architectural detail elements to complement any décor.

Note the small recessed spotlight, which has been installed in the ceiling of the niche. When creating art niches, you should always consider the lighting needed to showcase the contents.

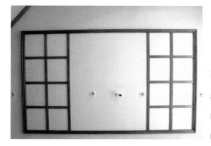

LEFT AND FAR LEFT ✢ On the ceiling, the flat crown was transformed by adding various molding styles: a 6-inch crown molding frames out the overall design. The final touch—the set of wooden trays installed as part of the center ceiling design.

6

FURNITURE DETAILS

It seems to me that designing detail furniture is what I was born to do; so much so that, for most of my career, my husband and I have operated a custom furniture manufacturing facility. The designs for my furniture line, the Mikala Collection, as well as the custom furniture pieces designed for my residential clients, all came to me in my sleep. The designs are visions of my dreams.

The special look of this night table is not found in its granite top, but rather in the ¾-inch thick glass that is sandwiched between the cabinet and the top. The chiseled front edge of the glass adds texture and movement to the top composition.

The cabinet base of the night table was designed with a recessed back to house a fluorescent light tube. (Note: The type of fluorescent I used is one that is suggested for the interior of cabinetry.) This light penetrates the glass, which gives the "wow!" to the design concept. When the fixture is switched on, the chiseled glass edge becomes a green glow. Additional detailing comes from the puzzle-cut drawer fronts, which allow the interior of the cabinet to maintain its storage function by keeping the interior a box shape. Large bullet-shaped cabinet pulls completed the composition. Only white drawer pulls were in stock, so I faux finished them in an antique copper finish. Nothing stops me when it comes to getting a finished look!

I WILL ADMIT right up front that most of the custom furniture and furniture details that I present in this chapter were designed by a professional: me. I believe it would be a major undertaking for you to create your own custom furniture and special details completely from scratch because it is necessary to have knowledge of scale, construction methods, available materials, and finishing techniques to design custom furnishings. This is specialized knowledge, which you may or may not possess yourself. However, if you have the budget and can find the right craftspeople, you can commission original furniture pieces, even of your own design.

All of the units featured in this chapter originated on paper as working drawings, which contain exact measurements, specifications for components, and diagrams for assembly. I have included exact working drawings, complete with all specs, for some of the custom furniture pieces featured in this chapter (beginning on page 172.) My hope is that you will see something that you love and flatter me by copying it. Even if you cannot use my exact designs, these drawings will help you create something similar and, I hope, inspire your own creative ideas. I recommend that you give the design to your architect, designer, or furniture maker, and have them create working drawings for your own custom piece.

THROUGH THE EYES OF CECIL

Furniture detailing, as with any other type of decorative detailing that you may choose to undertake, can be implemented in gradual installments. I believe that there is nothing wrong with decorating your home over a period of years. If anything, it makes the results even better. With time and thought, any home, regardless of size, can be made tasteful and charming. No one says you have to do it overnight!

HOME: AN ONGOING PROJECT

I feel that a home—be it yours or mine—is always an ongoing project. You may not make continuous design decisions, but over time you are bound to alter the décor, even if it is only superficially. I think one of the biggest mistakes that people can make is to rush into decorating—and this includes decorative detailing. It makes far more sense to take your time and get to know your home, your décor, and your lifestyle preferences. That way you can be assured that your finished look will be something you can live with.

My home is my design laboratory—it's always changing! Family and friends who visit me regularly swear that I change out the décor every year. This is categorically untrue . . . sort of. My husband, Powell, and I have enjoyed our home for more than sixteen years, and the changes that I have made, for the most part, have been changes to the decorative details.

One of my favorite furniture pieces is the entertainment and display unit in our family room. I designed the unit myself, and my husband fabricated and installed it when we first moved in. At the time, the box that housed the 36-inch large TV was the largest part of the unit. It still is. It is also the central cabinet, and visual center, of the unit.

ENTERTAINMENT AND WALL UNITS

Entertainment units are not a song-and-dance act, even if the items that they house—TVs and stereo equipment—entertain us. I feel very strongly that the cabinet itself must also give us visual pleasure. After all, when watching the TV we are also viewing the unit. For this reason the design and details must make the heart sing.

Here are some general rules to consider for entertainment unit design. Please take a few moments to think about them.

- ✤ "Stand-alone" TV and stereo equipment is not good décor.
- ✤ Decorative furnishings (chairs, sofas, consoles, etc.) and entertainment units do not mix well on the same wall.
- ✤ You must know the size of all equipment that will go in it before you can design the unit.
- ✤ It is critical that you know the best location for TV/stereo equipment before designing speaker locations.
- ✤ For proper viewing, you must consider the size of TV screen in relation to the size of the room.
- ✤ Storage needs must be assessed (including DVD, tapes, and CDs) before designing the unit.
- ✤ The cabinet area that houses audio equipment may need to be vented, or require a fan.

About four years ago, I was ready for a change. I realized I could make a significant change to my TV unit's look by making one simple design detail change—by merely adding molding around the TV cabinet frame. After it was installed, we were amazed at what a difference that small detail made. Our family and friends thought we had made a major change, and all it took was a simple touch. The photograph at top shows the TV cabinet/entertainment unit in my family room as I originally designed it.

THROUGH THE EYES OF CECIL

Style, architectural detailing, display, and entertainment can all be enjoyed on one wall, but the starting point for this multifunctional design begins with the furniture layout. This is a very important point. For best results, you must lay out your seating arrangements first. It's the seating arrangement, which dictates the location of the TV. Once you know which wall will house the TV, you can determine the other components in your design.

Although most of these rules are self-explanatory, there are two that I feel need further elaboration:

1. "Stand-alone" TV and stereo equipment is not good décor ✠ TV and stereo units are what I call "heavy metal." The look is functional, not haute design. While there are some units that have been designed for high-tech décor, the majority of them are still purely functional pieces of equipment. Remember, your home will be filled with beautiful furniture, accessories and art. If not concealed, this high-tech equipment in your living room, family room, or bedroom detracts from the glamor of the room's interior design. Of course, there are exceptions to every rule—high-tech décor, which accommodates mounted stand and units of minimal design quite well.

2. Decorative furnishings and entertainment units do not mix well on the same wall ✠ Mixing an equipment unit with other decorative items (i.e., design partners) is all about balance and scale. Let's say the entertainment wall in your den is 14 feet long. Your equipment, however, only requires a unit that is 3 feet long. It's not good design to place a 3-foot unit in the middle of a 14-foot wall. The ratio of unit to wall is unbalanced. Unfortunately, solving the problem requires more than placing a chair on either side of the unit. For one thing, the entertainment unit is too tall to act as a console or buffet. So what do you do?

You incorporate your entertainment equipment into a large-scale wall unit with design partners. The design partners that work best with equipment/entertainment units are bookcases, display cabinets, desks, bars, or just plain storage units. When using design partners in conjunction with entertainment units, realize that they become part of the unit design. The entire combined unit works best when it is at least three-quarters of the length of the wall.

One of my clients had an oceanfront condominium on the thirty-sixth floor. The space had an awesome view. Given the modern décor, a minimal TV treatment was perfect. There was only one place to locate the TV—in front of the bed (which also meant in front of the ocean view). In order to preserve the ocean view, we mounted a stainless steel TV and DVD stand to a small wall next to the large picture window. The client's view from the bed could encompass both the ocean and the TV at the same time.

Located in a small room, this large entertainment unit is a reflection of beauty. The unit is adorned with French doors on the front and sides, and the open frame doors are backed with mirror. The combination of mirrored doors and upper display areas lighten the load of the room. The unit itself is made of maple, which has been stained in a medium-tone brown.

DESIGNING THE PERFECT ENTERTAINMENT UNIT ✠ The perfect entertainment unit can be many things in many different settings. Ultimately, designing the perfect unit is about creating a focal point that adds style and charm to the setting. (For more information on general furniture arrangements, including additional tips and techniques for obtaining perfect furniture-to-wall balance, please see *9 Steps to Beautiful Living: Dream, Design and Decorate your Home with Style*.)

THROUGH THE EYES OF CECIL

The thing to know about all wall units is that they are a collection of boxes. Without special detailing, a wall unit can look just like a stack of those boxes. Detailing, however, is what really adds decorative interest!

THROUGH THE EYES OF CECIL

I suggest that you consider using about one-third of your entertainment cabinet as display. This ratio of design can be used for any size unit, even one that is very large. When a unit is 6 feet tall, or taller, the weight of the piece appears to be concentrated at its base. For this reason, display shelves are perfect for use on the upper portion of the unit. This open concept of display at the upper portion of the cabinet will give a lighter appearance to the overall

In this oceanfront condominium, the details of the overall installation were all about picking up the key architectural structures and using them within the existing floor plan. There are five large, round structural columns located in various places throughout the unit. Half of the round column shares the interior space; the others appear on the exterior balcony. This round column inspired the round cabinet that houses the TV and stereo equipment, and which visually connects the living and family room spaces. It was constructed with a center section, that swivels, allowing the TV to be viewed from either the living room or the den.

FULL WALL INSTALLATIONS ✤ Despite what you may think, entertainment units that cover entire walls will *not* make your room appear smaller. You can work them into architectural details in the room, continuing the lines of the unit into the lines of the structural elements.

REWORKING AN EXISTING INSTALLATION ✤ Many times in my career I have been commissioned to rework an existing installation, which always challenges me to look the furnishings and décor as they exist and imagine them in completely new ways. I've found that if you can see past what's familiar about something, see past its outer appearance and into its inner purpose, you can find a way to create a new design. I truly believe that a furniture item doesn't have to be new to become outstanding in a new way.

Of course, not every entertainment unit relies on the home's preexisting architectural details for its design concept. This entertainment unit was a plain unit before I added the molding. To give it character, the 2 ½-inch profile molding with a copper finish was cut into Aztec-inspired designs and applied to the white oak doors and drawers. The crown and foot of the unit were constructed in a V-cut design, keeping the focus of attention on the front of the piece. The large bullet-shaped pulls on the doors and drawers are another critical design detail. The copper finish accents the front of the cabinet, too, but the molding defines the design. (See page 172 for detailed working drawing of this entertainment unit.)

If I had to give a brief description for this design, it would be "a contemporary entertainment unit for a contemporary room." Those simple words, however, cannot convey its sophisticated style. The home décor was very important to both the design, and the detail, of the large entertainment unit. The unit is all about simple line design—no curves or carved molding. The sophistication is provided by the design detail of the changing hues of gray lacquer that are used. The body of the unit was lacquered with dawn gray, a medium shade. The flat molding, which accents both the shelves and the soffit, is of a lighter gray tone. Display shelves were then cantilevered from the TV cabinet, a detail that creates a lighter overall appearance, despite the large size of the unit. (See page 172 for detailed working drawing of this entertainment unit.)

The wall and the entertainment unit in this home are merged together into a single visual composition. The 16-foot wall was recessed 28 inches in order to accept the depth of the stereo/TV cabinets. The unit itself is covered in cherrywood, detailed with black accent wood that trims the upper center shelves and the TV cabinet. (See page 172 for detailed working drawing of this entertainment unit.)

This family room wall unit is a perfect example of how furniture doesn't have to be new to become outstanding. The unit already existed, and we weren't planning to change out the audio/visual equipment. What we were planning to do, however, was rework the unit to make it match the new room design concept. Originally, the entertainment unit was surrounded—on both sides and at the top—by black draperies. The original owner found this to be great for light control when watching TV, but, to me, it was depressing in the extreme. The new window treatment (see detail photo) allows enough natural light into the room to brighten it, but not so much that it interferes with TV viewing. In the new design, the entertainment unit, windows, and walls work hand in hand as detail partners. The original wall unit was a white-washed oak, refinished on site with a clear, natural oak finish to suit the new décor.

THROUGH THE
EYES OF CECIL

Continuous lines always enlarge the appearance of a room. For example, if you are a petite 5-feet-tall person, you always appear taller in a long, fitted evening dress. Conversely, a short dress with a belt at the waist makes you appear shorter. Similarly, small items on large walls top the eye at each item. This makes the visual more compact instead of one continuous flow.

BUFFETS, DESKS, NIGHT TABLES, VANITIES, CLOSETS, AND STORAGE UNITS

Opportunities for decorative detailing abound. I've added details to more furniture pieces than I can possibly describe in this chapter. To me, it's all about finding new materials and new ways to use existing materials that give one-of-a-kind detailing to furniture pieces.

BUFFET UNITS ✠ Strictly speaking, a buffet is a cupboard or sideboard used for storing dishes and serving food. Over the years, I designed many custom units for my clients' dining and breakfast rooms. This piece of furniture is one of the workhorses of family life. I believe that each and every design, however, should be as beautiful as it is functional. For more unusual buffet units, see Chapter 8.

I refer to this buffet as a design in ¾ round. The unit is attached to the wall on one side and the remaining three sides of the unit sit in the middle of the floor. This particular unit acts as a room divider for the dining room and dinette areas; its depth allows storage on both sides. The detailing is about mixing wood and metal. The square design detail on the doors and sides adds a note of sophistication. The square is bevel cut and its edges are trimmed with maple. The maple door pulls become part of the detail, too. They play up the straight-line design of the unit, and add detail to the raised panels of the unit.

DESKS ✤ Desks are another popular piece of furniture that I use in most of my decorative installations. Whether creating a custom design, using a cherished family antique, or repurposing a found unit, a desk is a practical addition to a home office or den. The style and size of the unit will be largely determined by the needs of the homeowner.

NIGHT TABLES ✤ Night tables are among those furniture items that everybody can use. They are a practical necessity, normally placed on one or both sides of the bed. In the bedroom they hold lamps, alarm clocks, telephones, books, drinks, etc. I've designed a variety of them in various sizes and finishes over the years. This is one item that is readily available to the consumer in prices to fit every budget. Like other, larger pieces of furniture, night tables can benefit from decorative detailing.

Sometimes the end is the beginning. This theory is true of a contemporary desk unit in a recent installation. The body of the desk unit, which includes top, storage, and shelves, is a basic design. But, the end panel of the desk is a carved, tiered design made of wood. In this case, the end of the unit design was the beginning of a great look.

THROUGH THE
EYES OF CECIL

Bathrooms are rooms. Detail them with the same accessories that you would use in other rooms: paintings, flowers, area rugs, and other art items can all be used with aplomb!

BATHROOM VANITIES ✣ Designers and architects have noted that the bathroom can be a major asset when buying or selling your home. Not only that, it's the first room we enter in the morning and the next to last room we enter at night. In this hardworking room, vanity style and design can make for an eye-catching interior. Vanities add so much value to a look because they are furniture items, and they can be designed and detailed with an endless variety of materials ranging from wood to plastic. The detail on the doors and drawers of a vanity are stand-alone furniture designs. In other words, to design a vanity you love, you don't have to be concerned with how the piece mixes with other items, as you would in a living room installation. I think bath vanity areas should be defined as areas where beautiful things happen.

The master vanity in this luxury bath is 10 feet long and milady's dressing table is included in its length. The cabinet itself is made of mahogany. Design details are found in three areas of the unit: (1) The molding on the doors and drawers are trimmed with silver leaf; (2) the base is an open curved stainless steel stand; and (3) the end of the vanity has open storage for rolled hand towels.

POWDER BATHS ✣   Powder baths come in all sizes, shapes, and design aesthetics. One thing that you can always count on, however, is the predominance of striking vanity design. The powder bath vanity, as the central furniture item in the room, is an immensely powerful vehicle for decorative detail.

THROUGH THE EYES OF CECIL

In a powder bath, little or no storage capacity is required of the vanity design. What is required, however, is unforgettable design detailing. Since the powder bath is the only room in a home that requires a short stay, you can use your powder bath to make your most daring statements. It's all about those very few minutes of viewing.

It's the doors on this cabinet that define the style of my clients' powder bath. The overall design style is traditional, with heavily carved wood in a leaf motif to supply the detail. Looking at it now, you would never know that the original vanity design called for plain wood doors. With a little research, however, I found a company that specialized in carved wood motifs (see Sources for more information). From the wide variety of sizes available, I was able to select the right size motif to balance the doors. It is very important to the finished product that the applied motif doesn't appear to be applied. The doors must look as if they were carved from solid pieces of wood, and here we have been very successful in creating that effect.

In this project, I was faced with a closet problem—specifically, lack of closet space in a condominium unit. While the master bedroom did have one large walk-in closet, this space was insufficient.

The moment I entered this bedroom, I recognized that we had enough space to create additional storage. The wall immediately adjacent to bed wall was 14 feet long, not including the adjoining 6-foot window. The wall was too long for just a 36-inch TV wall unit, which is all the clients had requested. It would have looked totally out of proportion to the space. But, if I created a 3-foot TV cabinet, that would leave me with 11 feet of wall, which I could use to create additional storage. I chose wood for the total storage/TV unit design in order to complement the existing space. Function truly can be beautiful, as this rich wood cabinet so successfully demonstrates.

DETAIL UNITS FOR CLOSET STORAGE ✜ One of the most common problems I face in my design practice is my clients' perpetual need for more storage. I think this is true for just about everyone I meet. The old adage "a place for everything and everything in its place" is one of the true tenants for successful interior design, and nowhere is it more apparent than in creating additional storage space.

Most of my clients divide their time between two or more homes, making their stay in each approximately four to six months out of the year, yet they still feel a need for more storage. I, on the other hand, live in one home and I still need more storage for my stuff. If, like me, you have lots of stuff, don't put up the For Sale sign just yet. Nine times out of ten there is a detail concept that can help you out . . . and it costs a lot less than that remodel you're contemplating or that new home that you thought you needed.

RETHINKING YOUR STORAGE NEEDS ✤ Sometimes it is absolutely necessary to rethink and rework your storage options. Life, as we all know, is not static, and changing circumstances have direct impact on our storage needs. Whatever the challenge, with careful consideration and strategic planning you can meet most of your storage needs.

One of the most unusual furniture details that I have created is the sofa/TV unit for these clients. Created for their master bedroom, the design called for a TV hidden within the loveseat at the foot of the bed. With a touch of a button, the TV rises up from the back of the sofa, allowing the clients to enjoy watching TV in bed. When not in use, the unit is conveniently hidden within a piece of functional furniture.

MURPHY BEDS

Murphy beds have come a long way since the time Abbott and Costello used them as comedy gags. These days, Murphy beds are perfect for studio apartments, small guest rooms, and rooms that serve more than one function. The comfort of Murphy beds, in most cases, is far better than that of sofa sleepers. This is, in part, because sofa sleeper mattresses are made thin to allow them to fold into the sofa frame. Murphy bed mattresses, on the other hand, are standard mattresses—8 to 13 inches deep. Additionally, Murphy bed units take up far less room space, since they are only 14 to 18 inches deep; sleeper sofas are 36 inches deep.

The Murphy bed designs shown here are all located in what I call multipurpose rooms. The main function of the space dictates the look of the décor. The concealed Murphy bed must take a positive stand in appeal and style and reflect the overall décor of the room. Murphy beds also work well with design partners like bookshelves and shallow cabinets.

The original bedroom space in this home (12 feet x 14 feet) now functions primarily as a home office, for which I created a custom-built desk and storage cabinet, which makes for a perfect work area. Once or twice a year, however, the space doubles as a bedroom for holiday guests. To accommodate guests, we installed a Murphy bed unit, which houses two twin beds. The unit itself is veneered with the same book-match walnut as the desk and storage cabinet, and is further defined by the wood inlay design. To complete the detail concept, the Murphy bed unit is finished with bookshelves.

This cabana guest house also services a covered patio/pool area. 12-foot glass doors slide into pockets into the wall, which allow the space to be a part of the outdoor entertainment. The décor is tropical, in colors of cool blue and hot yellow. The Murphy bed is in an island design. Woven grass-cloth and white oak-wood trim were applied to the doors and drawers. Custom door pulls are large in scale to balance the doors. They also serve a second purpose: they give a good grip for pulling the bed down to the floor. (See page 173 for detailed working drawing of this Murphy bed.)

THROUGH THE EYES OF CECIL

To design furniture that has that "set aside" look, you must be fearless with your detailing. You should boldly change the purpose or intended use of your accent materials; woven leather is a great example of this concept. Originally intended for upholstery, I have used it as an inset in the drawer front of an unusual night table.

LET'S REVIEW

There's nothing wrong with taking your time creating your space. Sometimes the best interiors take years to develop. Such has been the case in my own home. Since I use it like a design laboratory, my personal interior is always changing. Don't be afraid to experiment with decorative details at your home, either.

One of the ways that you can achieve maximum design impact in your home is by creating your own custom furnishings and adding personalized decorative detailing both with them, and to them. Internet searches and magazines pages are great places to look for pieces that inspire you and that you can then have created by a professional cabinetmaker. Some of the most common decorative furnishing elements include:

- Buffets
- Closets
- Desks
- Entertainment units
- Murphy bed units
- Storage cabinets
- Vanities

Opportunities for decorative detailing for furnishings abound. It's all about finding new materials and new ways to use existing materials to give one-of-a-kind detailing to furniture pieces.

In this installation, lacquer, leather, glass, and metal come together to create a fabulous detail design. The body was a simple rectangular box. The detailing began with four triangular-shaped stands, 2½ inches high, which support the painted red glass top. Like the stands, the drawer fronts are lacquered wood. Inlaid woven leather panels provide additional detailing on the drawer front while stainless steel pulls complete the mix. The result: a slick contemporary design. (See page 173 for detailed working drawing of this night table.)

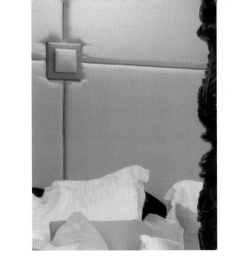

7

FABRIC AND SOFT COVERING DETAILS

I know I keep coming back to it, but detailing is not about cost. It's all about creating details that

look like a million bucks using just your big ideas!

FABRIC AND SOFT trims are one of the biggest spurs to decorative detailing that I can imagine. They can be used in more ways than you can count, on everything from walls, to furnishings, to throw pillows with fabulous results. One reason that I find fabric irresistible is its sheer versatility. Think about it: Fabric can be sewed, glued, stapled, cut, shaped, appliquéd, draped, and otherwise manipulated. It comes in so many colors, textures, and decorative finishes that it makes this designer feel like a kid in the proverbial candy shop!

There is versatility in using fabric and fabric-covered items to create decorative detailing. I use it to create decorative details in:

✥ Accessories
✥ Bedding
✥ Skirted tables
✥ Upholstery

Upholstered walls are appropriate for use with any design style. Not only do they make fabulous headboard features, they are excellent at playing up existing furnishings. In one client's very traditional home, the wall space directly behind the headboard reflected the bed canopy. Dupioni silk was upholstered on four square panels that framed the four-poster walnut bed. A three-dimensional square button adds the perfect center detail.

To be successful, it is not necessary that you choose fabric that grabs you by the throat and slings you around to gain attention. Often, it can be the subtle tone-on-tone change of texture that adds a touch of opulence to a finished interior. You can also get detail mileage by layering fabrics and playing off textures against one another. The trick, however, is in knowing when enough is just right.

TRADE SECRET

BEDDING

Bedding is one of the easiest, and most readily available, decorative uses for fabric. Because the bed is usually the largest item in the room, it makes sense that the bedding would represent the most dominant pattern in the bedroom décor—it's your opportunity to really make a statement. Bedding is very versatile and can be handled in a variety of ways.

MIX IT UP ✤ This technique is pretty much exactly what it sounds like: mixing various fabrics and textures together to adorn the bed. I have used this technique throughout my career, often installing as many as six different fabric toppers (not including the sheets) in the bedroom for a look that is voluptuously comfortable and inviting.

The goal, in this case, is to make bedding the center of attention, and most of your mainstream department stores display this kind of creative detailing. In fact, linen designers have done such a great job mixing and matching a variety of fabrics that you may just want to shop for the look you seek. Believe me, there are many, many great looks readily available on the market. If you don't want to fuss to make a bed look beautiful every day, then this may not be the look for you. But you are missing out on a great look, which will make you feel refreshed each and every day.

Blue and white are perennial favorites, and this bedroom, with its study of patterns and textures, is no exception. The blue floral patterns used throughout the room are complemented by the solid white matelisse bed topper and pillow sham fabrics, as well as the white table cover. The small blue-and-white pattern in the wallpaper reads almost as a solid, as does the blue-on-blue floral design in the bed skirt. The largest pattern in the room is in the floor rug, and it is subtly echoed on the creamy headboard. Touches of yellow throughout the room keep the blue-and-white décor from seeming too cold. Design and photo © Waverly

ADDING SOFT TRIMS ✤ Soft trims are fabric-based trim items, such as bullion and other fringes, braid, tassels, and bindings. Because they are fabric based, these trims are soft to the touch (hence the name "soft trim"). Soft trims work best in situations where they won't get a lot of regular handling, such as on window treatments, throw pillows, and table cloths and runners. Because bedspreads and duvet covers are handled every day when the bed is made and unmade, and because many people sleep under them, I don't recommend applying any trim to them that is easy to pull off or may offer cleaning nightmares. (Sitting or sleeping on top of beautiful bedding is bad bed etiquette, per my mother.) If you do decide to use trims on duvets and bedspreads, for the best results, select a trim that is tightly woven and smooth or flat.

CREATING A TURN-BACK ✤ The artfully made bed is a prominent feature in home décor magazines these days. As a designer, I love the decorative possibilities of this look because it's one way to incorporate a variety of textiles into the room décor. I'm especially fond of adding decorative turn-backs to the bedscape, and have employed them in my own home for many years.

If you really want to add a unique accessory to your bedding, you can easily create your own turn-back. In the old days, this was a decorative item that showcased the household's best needlework, but today you aren't limited to hand-worked linen, or anything else for that matter. Just find a fabric with some length that fits right into your design concept and use it to create your look. Some examples are scarves, throws, folded quilts, or a length of any fabric that appeals to you. I especially like the look of a vintage lace tablecloth. When paired with a bevy of beautiful throw pillows, the look—no matter which topper you choose—is simply beautiful.

CREATING A DECORATIVE HEMLINE ⌘ Creating a decorative hemline refers to the addition of details meant to add interest and draw attention to the hem. These details may be as subtle or flamboyant as you wish. While they can be applied to a bed skirt or bedspread, creating a decorative hem can also be much more than that. Have you ever thought about applying hem details to the bed frame itself? If you have a fully upholstered bed frame, there is certainly no reason why you can't consider this treatment.

In this client's home the fully upholstered bed frame and unusual headboard treatment set the stage for this chalet bedroom. Here, we created a decorative hemline using two unique details: 12-inch twisted rope fringe and 2-inch wood molding installed above the fringe. The molding divides the frame height. It is also a detail element of the tile headboard.

HEADBOARDS AND CANOPIES

In addition to bedding selection, there are other opportunities for decorative detailing in the bedroom centered on the bed—upholstered headboards and canopies. Often associated with traditional décor, upholstered headboards have recently become popular in contemporary and transitionally styled homes as well. Beautiful bedrooms, whatever the style aesthetic, rely heavily upon fabric treatments and trims.

UPHOLSTERED HEADBOARDS ✠ Upholstered headboards have been around for decades and offer many opportunities for detailing, which range from layering fabrics to adding decorative trims such as welting and cording, and additional embellishments such as buttons and tufting, to the design. I prefer understated upholstery when it comes to bed frames and headboards. By this, I mean that I like the trims to peacefully blend with the upholstery.

When you don't want to completely change out your headboard, but long for some kind of change, consider slipcovering. A slipcover, as in upholstery, is a temporary fabric covering. It can be as simple as draping the headboard with a beloved quilt or other textile, or creating a tailored tie-on treatment. Slipcovers are meant to be temporary, so let your imagination run free!

CANOPY BEDS ✠ A canopy can be as straightforward as a length of fabric draped across a series of curtain rods that have been mounted to the ceiling, or as complicated as a four poster with full drapery treatment and upholstered canopy. The looks are as varied as the people who live with them.

The classic canopy gets the full treatment in this master bedroom. The bed, with its red hangings in a bold medallion print, takes center stage. The floral duvet cover and soft gold walls tone down the vibrant reds and large-scale patterns. Design and photo © Waverly

When I look at bed detailing, I see it as romantic, or jazzy/exotic. Romantic to me equates soft fabrics and small patterns. Jazzy/exotic, on the other hand, is a bold mixing of colors, patterns, and textures.

The gold upholstery fabric is the perfect foil to this blue bedroom with its soft floral drapes, duvet cover, and throw pillows. Extremely subtle detailing on this upholstered bed frame includes single welting at the base of the head- and footboards. Carved molding finishes off the side rail.

UPHOLSTERY

Upholstery is another great way to bring fabric detailing into any room. If you are the adventurous sort, you can try your hand at full-scale upholstery; or perhaps hire a professional to upholster at your direction.

If you choose to try it yourself, there is a wealth of information available on the subject in magazines, books, and on the Internet. You may also wish to check out some of your local continuing education classes—often you can find an upholstery class in your area.

If you do choose to go it alone, be certain to do two things: (1) Make detailed notes on the order in which the piece of furniture was disassembled, and notes on its construction, to use for re-assembly; and (2) use the old fabric pieces to create patterns for your new fabric before you discard them. The upholstery process can be overwhelming for the novice, so take my advice and start small. It can be done, however, so don't despair. My parents reupholstered several pieces when I was growing up, and I know that neither of them had formal training. They just had common sense and Mother's sewing skills.

When you are looking for a simple, easy method to detail an item, try using fabric and trims. You can twist them, sew them, glue them, etc. Hand-work is in, and it gives a personal touch to your décor.

The upholstery on this balloon-backed chair uses a color blocking approach to upholstery. The back of the chair is blue, while the seat and arms are green. Since green and blue are next to one another on the color wheel, this analogous pairing is easy on the eye.

UPHOLSTERED DINING CHAIRS ✥ One of the easiest and least intimidating applications is to create details on your dining chairs. Oftentimes only the seat of the chair is upholstered, and changing that fabric is a simple process. Another advantage for the beginner is that, window treatment not included, the dining chairs usually contain the only fabric used in the dining room, which may simplify the fabric selection process somewhat.

In dining rooms with six or more chairs that are upholstered with two or more fabrics each, be sure to consider the overall look of the room. Keep in mind that walls and window coverings look best in solids or small prints.

UPHOLSTERED CHAIRS ✥ You can customize a chair by matching it with coordinates, adding a skirt design to an existing chair, removing a skirt in favor of decorative trim, welt, back, pillow back, changing colors of seat cushions, etc. One special chair in a room may be all the detail needed if you match it up with fabrics that coordinate with the room's existing décor.

With chairs that are a combination of upholstery and wood framing, the frame that separates the chair back from the seat and the seat from the arms means the fabrics never meet. It's easy to mix fabric on chairs like these, whether in the living room or dining room. Mixing fabric on a chair is like creating your own fabric pattern design. Take extra care to secure an exact color match, so shop it out and match as you go. One of the easiest ways to secure an exact color match is to depend upon fabric swatch books with coordinates. If mixing prints on chairs is not your look—don't print it, color it! Using different colors on the back, seat, and arms of your chair(s) is also a special detail.

ADDING DETAILING WITH WELT

Welt (or welting) is fabric that is sewn over cord. It is round and comes in several standard sizes ($\frac{1}{4}$ inch, $\frac{1}{2}$ inch, and $1\frac{1}{2}$ inch are most commonly used). Welting is generally used to trim upholstery seams and places where fabric meets exposed wood and can be single or double. (Single welt is one cord. Double welt is two parallel cords.) Welt can also be used as edging on draperies, bedspreads, table linen, etc. As a decorative accent, welt has a lower price point than manufactured fringes and trims. Welt is small in size, but it can twist and wrap itself into an appealing detail design.

A pair of brown suede armchairs in my client's family room feature loose cushions in white leather, which are further detailed with chocolate brown welt trim. The overall impression is striking!

THROUGH THE EYES OF CECIL

Simple white cotton slipcovers dress the dining chairs. The understated accents include white buttons down the back and inverted pleats at the front corners of each chair. Design and photo © Waverly

SLIPCOVERS

Mention slipcovers and everyone automatically thinks of the loose-fitting covers used on sofas and armchairs. The truth of the matter is that there is nothing to stop you from creating slipcovers to adorn dining chairs. Armless chairs are quite easy to slipcover, regardless of whether you prefer a simple fitted slipcover or something more elaborate.

Armchairs are a little more difficult, although there is nothing to stop you from creating fitted slipcovers to adorn the backs or even to cover the entire chair if you should so choose. And, of course, you can always hire a professional to create your slipcovers. Most fabric stores will be able to refer to you to qualified and reliable professionals.

SKIRTED TABLES

What is underneath the covering of a skirted table is no one's business . . . and we really don't care because the beauty of this decorative detail in the covering, not what's being covered. The fabric choice will dictate the look of the skirted table. Table skirt fabrics can be small, medium, or large patterns, or even combinations of all three. For the most part, skirted tables are round in shape, but you'll occasionally see skirts that are square, or other shapes.

Who says tablecloths are just for indoor use? This combination pairs a large-scale floral topper over a stripe underskirt. Acrylic fabrics can stand up to the weather, and the bolder patterns and colors won't seem as overpowering outdoors. Design and photo © Waverly

THROW PILLOWS

I sincerely hope that throw pillows are never removed from a stylish décor, since nothing can carry off a design detail better than a throw pillow. For me, taking throw pillows out of décor would be like removing makeup from all the stores. How could I possibly perk up a look without either lipstick or a pillow? The thought is enough to give any designer nightmares!

Now, many of my client's don't like a lot of pattern or what they call a busy room. I, on the other hand, don't want the completed room to be lacking in excitement. So, I have found a way to blend the best of both worlds: throw pillows. Throw pillows with prints or pattern, throw pillows with bows and beads, throw pillows with feathers—the options are endless. I look at the throw pillows themselves as design details. If you don't believe me, remove the pillows from your sofa or bed (or if you don't have any, try adding some) and you will see what I mean.

Go wild at throw-pillow time. The fabric detailing options are endless. Mixing patterns, twisting, gathering, pleating, pinching—all of these techniques make for creative applications. Throw pillows can be your personal one-of-a-kind, made-it-myself accent pieces.

Throw pillows are easy to fabricate or to alter to suit your needs. Pillow fills are sold in local fabric stores and come in several types: Dacron, down, feather/down combinations, foam rubber chips, or cotton batting. (Personally, I prefer down fills.) If you don't sew, you can purchase ready-made throw pillows and then add your own embellishments.

How many throw pillows should one use on sofas or beds? There is no magic number. Take the size of the bed and sofa and make sure the pillows balance the size of the unit. For example, I have placed only two throw pillows on twin beds and as many as ten pillows on king-sized beds. What we do know is that two pillows on a king bed is just wrong.

On a sofa, be reasonable with the amount of pillows because you have to have room to sit on it. End of sofas and corners of L-shaped sofas are good locations to rest pillows. In my thinking, any seating that is not used day-to-day should be covered with throw pillows; when guests visit, just remove the pillows. After all, it is called a throw pillow. Throw it on the floor, if you need to.

TRADE SECRET

The decorator karate chop is one of the best designer secrets I know. Just a simple karate chop to the top of a throw pillow fluffs it out, perks it up, and gives it that "lived in" appeal. Whenever you set a throw pillow, don't forget "our little secret." Otherwise your pillow arrangements will look too pristine and contrived.

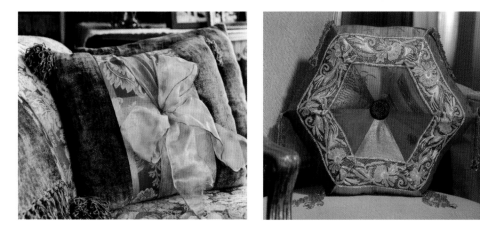

LEFT ✤ Beautiful throw pillows are easier to make than you might think. Use this no-sew concept to dress up plain chenille throw pillows: Wrap pillows with an extra-wide fabric ribbon, then wrap with organdy ribbon and finish off with a large bow.

RIGHT ✤ If you sew or have access to a seamstress, spectacular throw pillows are literally at your fingertips. Beautiful creations, such as this hexagonal pillow, can be created from a variety of fabrics, trims, and tassels. In this instance, a variety of silk fabrics were combined with beaded trim and tassels.

THROUGH THE EYES OF CECIL

If something looks "good" in an interior décor, it probably didn't occur by accident. The same holds true for throw pillows. Pillows arranged on a sofa should not be lined up on edge like soldiers, but at the same time they should also appear soft and inviting. This is why a soft fill is preferable. It's nice, soft, and holds its shape beautifully. Down is the best fill to give that decorator karate chop to!

✤ Use handmade fabric rosettes.

✤ Cut a striped fabric in quarters and then turn the stripes ¼ turn each to create geometric boxes.

✤ Appliqué a pattern cut from a print onto a solid fabric background.

✤ Use patchwork (you must love the look of quilts for this one).

✤ Use two fabrics, one as a background and the other as a pleated decorative band.

✤ Apply fabric that has been sheared on both long sides of the pillow.

✤ Make use of buttons covered with different fabric colors and textures.

✤ Sew two colors together to make a design.

✤ Use torn fabric as fringe for all four corners.

✤ Try a creative juxtaposition of different textures.

✤ Try bag-tied corners on your prepurchased pillow.

✤ Apply 3-inch diameter silk flowers to a pillow top.

These are just a few creative concepts. I'm sure that if you think about it you can come up with many more! The amount of time and money you spend to create your own designer throw pillows is actually very little when you consider that its impact on the décor is priceless.

Use throw pillows to further accent a décor. A variety of patterns, textures, fabrics, and trims can be combined onto different throw pillows, such as these in this sofa grouping. Occasionally, I like to vary the shape of the pillows themselves for added interest.

If you are thinking for one minute to use the same trims and fabrics for all the pillows, forget it! I say make the look more collectible. Make them all different. To have all the pillows covered with the same fabric or trims is safe and proper. To use different coverings on pillows is exciting, creative, and fun . . . so live dangerously!

ACCESSORIES

In my mind, accessory details are one of the best places to use fabrics and soft trims. You don't need much to add oomph to your décor. I like to see them used in unexpected places: lampshades, picture frames, and small wall treatments, for example.

LAMPSHADES ✤ Lampshades remind me of hats because of the many different decorative ornaments that can be applied to them. In fact, if I am ever at a loss for how to adorn a lampshade, or, simply looking for inspiration, I go right to the most fabulous source of millinery that I can find—the British royal family. I confess right now that I try to catch all the news about them that I can, not because I am a dedicated Anglophile, but because I love their hats! Simple or fancy, they are always part of any affair attended by royals, and they are always fabulous accents to the ladies' ensembles. Similarly, there is a lady who attends my church, who changes the ornamentation on her hat on any given Sunday. I don't always like the look, but you have to admire her creative spirit!

I think smart lampshades are one of the best accents for any home décor. Simple or simply fantastic, the shade on a lamp can be the perfect decorative detail that ties your look together. You can adorn shades in many ways: Add fabric and beads, use fabric that matches your upholstery, add fabric and feathers, try sheer fabrics, use theme fabrics (for children's rooms, etc.), and much, much more. And, you can create it yourself by either embellishing an existing shade or making something entirely from scratch.

A stunning lampshade from the hands of artisan Christine Kilger. This one-of-a-kind shade is made of vintage fabrics, metallic trims, millinery flowers, and decorative hand embroidery. The finished creation was then hand-beaded. At right, a close-up view of the fabulous fabrics and trims used to create this spectacular shade.

Meticulous hand-beading is one of the trademarks of Christine Kilger's handmade lampshades.

This vintage table lamp sports a scimitar-shaped shade with elaborate beaded trim.

A wooden picture frame can be easily embellished with the aid of some paint, decorative ribbons in various colors, and the beads of your choice. Not into beads? Try buttons, charms, even silk flowers, instead!

PICTURE FRAMES ✣ Using picture frames to display your favorite photos is a timeless decorating strategy. But how about detailing your collection of frames? Though it's not something that you see every day, it can have tremendous design impact, whether your frames are displayed on a side table or hung on the wall.

Vintage lace glued to a plain wooden frame can create a wonderful decorative detail. Or you could look to vintage millinery materials to create velvet ribbon flowers to glue to the frame. You might upholster your frames in coordinating fabrics, or maybe use custom welting or soft trims to adorn the edges of the frames. All of these simple and inexpensive treatments can yield fantastic detail results.

Perhaps you want to create custom mats to set off your pictures. You can use fabric and trims. Ribbons, laces, feathers, even charms can be used to create one-of-a-kind picture matting. After all, creative detailing is not about cost—it's about creating a million-dollar look with the budget at hand, and that's where your big ideas can save you lots of money. Of course, you can also make your ideas work on a larger scale, too. Large mirror frames covered with fabric are another great look.

LET'S REVIEW

Fabric and soft trims can be used to create a myriad of decorative details. Fabric is a highly versatile material. It can be sewed, glued, stapled, cut, shaped, and otherwise manipulated, and it is excellent for creating decorative details in:

- ⁜ Accessories
- ⁜ Bedding
- ⁜ Skirted tables
- ⁜ Throw pillows
- ⁜ Upholstery

All of the above details can be created by layering multiple fabrics, combining patterns and textures, combining materials with decorative stitching, and adding soft trims. Decorative detailing doesn't have to be over-the-top. Often, an understated application can have just as much impact on the finished décor.

Of all of the areas where you can use decorative detailing, bedding is probably one of the easiest to install. There are so many beautiful bed ensembles available, it can be as simple as purchasing one that you love. Of course, there is no rule that says you can't add further decorative embellishment to these purchased items. Hem treatments immediately come to mind and may be easy to achieve. Another option is to add a decorative turn-back to the bedding, which may take the form of a scarf, throw, or even folded quilt across the head or foot of the bed. Then of course, there are the decorative throw pillows. Whether complementary or contrasting in style, I love to use them abundantly!

Upholstery is another area where fabric detailing can have fabulous results. There is no hard-and-fast rule that says you must use the same fabric on every surface of an upholstered item. If it will work in your décor, why not use a combination of materials and trims? Even such subtle trim as self-welt can have dramatic impact. If full-scale upholstery is not an option, slipcovers may be the right approach. These can be simple or elaborate and offer the perfect canvas for unusual combinations of fabrics and trims. Best of all, slipcovers can be made for anything from headboards to buffet tables and side tables to sofas and armchairs.

Table-toppers are a great addition to your decorative detail wardrobe. Aside from the fact that they can be easily removed and cleaned, they can be readily changed out for differing effect. Another advantage is that the yardage requirements are small, generally allowing the budget to stretch to several toppers. Decorative accessories, including throw pillows, lampshades, and picture frames offer further opportunities for decorative enhancement.

8

TRANSFORMATION IMAGINATION

I'm a firm believer that decorative detailing sparks the imagination and helps you visualize old things in new ways. I also believe that the very act of transforming objects and rooms through decorative detailing sparks the imagination of all who view them. This is what I call transformation imagination.

I THINK THERE are two primary ways that decorative details inspire imagination: (1) when transforming (or re-working) a found object and (2) when creating a theme-oriented environment. Transforming or reworking an object is the process of either embellishing an existing item or using an existing item to create something with an entirely different purpose. Creating a themed environment uses decorative detailing to transform an entire room or area.

While each application (transformation vs. themed environment) is quite different from the other, they are similar in that the finished product is the result of using decorative detailing to spark the imagination.

FABULOUS FINDS TRANSFORMED

I think most of us have had this experience: We're out shopping or just looking around and we come across something that really intrigues us. We walk around with it for a few moments musing on it, wondering how we might use it. Then, we put it down with a sigh and walk away. After all, what would you do with a thing like that anyway? Well, I'm here to tell you why, next time, you should take that thing home with you. In transformation decorative detailing, finding a new purpose or decorative usage for an object that has caught your eye is the whole point, the wonderful challenge. It's all about taking creativity to the nth degree!

Just what kind of item is suitable for transformation? It can be as varied as a piece of furniture, a table leg, a carved horn spoon, or an unusual bead—literally anything

THE BIG SCREEN ✣ I have a fondness for carved screens and panels. Living as I do near a major port (Miami), I have many opportunities to acquire beautiful carved screens and panels. For this client, I created a one-of-a-kind headboard by combining three carved panels into the perfect decorative detail for a king-sized bed. The screens look to be hand-carved antiques of Indonesian origin. Asian, Indonesian, and South American importers often have access to such treasures, which you can use to create your own artistic design detail.

THROUGH THE EYES OF CECIL

THROUGH THE EYES OF CECIL

at all that really strikes your fancy. There is no end to the interesting items that you or I may come across in retail stores, flea markets, thrift stores, on the Internet, and even at yard sales.

There are two ways that you can transform a fabulous find: (1) a simple transformation, where you add decorative detailing to enhance the piece, without changing its function; and (2) a complete transformation, where your detailing completely transforms the piece and changes its purpose.

SIMPLE TRANSFORMATIONS: *Rethinking the Old and Familiar* ✠ In its simplest form, furniture transformation is about adding new elements to an existing piece in order to update the overall appearance, from simply changing hardware (e.g., door pulls) to adding molding to door and drawer panels. Simple transformations can involve adding new materials, subtracting existing ones, and making changes to color, finish, and texture.

The hunt for the right details to add to furniture pieces, at least for me, is not about shopping at all—it's about finding. You see, to me, to "shop" for a thing means that you know exactly what it is you want to buy and you go to buy it in a place that you know carries it. To "find" something, however, means just that. You come across it, often purely by accident, while looking for something else, or for nothing in particular. You shop in a specific store for a particular drawer pull you saw in a magazine, but you find antique cut-glass doorknobs at a flea market and realize they'd make great door pulls. I can't predict what exact object(s) will inspire your furniture detailing ideas; I just know that the more you look, the more inspired you'll be in finding unusual items and applications to dress up existing furniture.

How do you know when you've found the right decorative accent? You know that something is IT when it appears to you and, for some reason, will not leave your thoughts. Your imagination teems with possibilities, all of which revolve around IT.

Long experience has shown me that if you run across something that you *really* like, love, or find interesting, even if you don't know exactly what you'll do with it, *buy it*! (If you wait until you figure out how to use it, it probably won't still be there when you go back to buy it.) Since I don't believe in keeping a warehouse for objects for future detailing projects, I put a limit on the number of items I purchase spontaneously. And, once I do get it home, I make sure that I look at it at least once a week. (This is essential: If you will do that, sooner or later a great idea will be born!)

In each of the my furniture projects, some portion of the design was inspired or made even better by decorative detailing. From horn spoons, to wrought-iron railings, to daisy fabric (and everything in between), the clever use of unusual elements lifts the finished designs to even greater heights.

BUFFED UP ✣ Adding a terrific design detail to an existing item in your home is like finding new money. In my book, *9 Steps to Beautiful Living*, I shared my old Vitricor buffet story, and I am still very much in love with the way I altered the cabinet design, reinventing it three times. The original finish on the buffet top and doors was a plastic laminate known as Vitricor. In the first transformation (top), I upgraded the top to black granite. In the second transformation (center), I added decorative picture frame molding and brass lion head door pulls to the doors. The third, and maybe final (but why make rash promises!), transformation (bottom) was inspired by a fantastic find.

One day I was browsing in a store that specializes in African and Asian artifacts when I can upon my new door pulls. Now, mind you, what I found were not intended to be door pulls. In fact, I wasn't sure exactly what they were. Displayed on Lucite stands, they looked like the carved horn of a cow. The proprietor confirmed that they were indeed carved horn—more precisely, hand-carved Ethiopian spoons! The more I looked at them, the more convinced I became that they would make perfect door pulls—the durability of the horn, the outwardly curving shape, the sheer unexpectedness of using the spoons this way. Each pull is slightly different in size and carving, but I think that only adds to its originality. Being inspired by a cabinet door pull may appear to be a small thing, but the truth is that it made a very *big* difference and was a major change in the cabinet design.

WROUGHT WITH STYLE ⚜ One of the most unusual buffet treatments I ever created involved the use of wrought-iron ornamentation. Applied to the doors of a buffet, wrought-iron ornaments create a very rich, and certainly unexpected, appeal. Custom forged ironwork is expensive, however, so I put my wits to work to find a way to keep the costs down. I discovered that wrought-iron railing for gates and stair rails can be purchased by the part or component, at a much lower cost. On this buffet, the center portion of a stair railing fit perfectly on the cabinet doors, and made an arresting repeat motif. (If the railing hadn't fit on the door panels, I could have had them cut to fit.)

EXOTIC LOOKS ⚜ I used a combination of wrought iron and carved wood to detail another unusual buffet unit. Originally a plain ash wood, the simple unit screamed for decorative detailing. To begin, I installed simple "loops" of wrought iron as the supporting legs of the unit. Next, I came across a portion of a carved screen or carved pelmet at a local import shop. (I have never been quite certain what it originally was, or where it was from, because there was only part of it when I found it.) The unusual color of the paint, combined with the exotic carvings, inspired me to use it to detail a basic buffet cabinet. The screen/pelmet was cut into individual pieces just wide enough to adorn each door; they also serve as door pulls. The installation is certainly unusual, but it makes for unforgettable decorative detailing!

RAISED UP ✛ Many years ago, I purchased an earthy bench to put at the foot of my bed. (I call it "earthy" because it is complex, and covered with jute rope.) Once it was installed, the bench was a bit lower than I wanted, but I liked it so much that I used it anyway. Much later, when I added a Kilim runner rug to bring color and character into the room, I was inspired to design a wooden base to my too-low bench. The process was very simple: A rectangular box was made about ¼ inch larger than the original bench and about 2½ inches high (which brought the original bench to the perfect height for sitting). Using oil-based paint, I painted triangular shapes on the wood box to mimic the carpet motif. The legs of the original bench were then screwed onto the new base for stability.

HANDLE IT ✛ Everyone is familiar with purchased hardware—e.g., doorknobs and door handles. It comes in various sizes, shapes, and finishes, but can you use it to create something new and exciting? Well, not long ago, a plain chrome door handle inspired me! This simple curved handle came in various sizes from 2 inches to 8 inches in length, all of which were illustrated in the supplier's catalog, one under another from small to large. I remember thinking, "If they were reversed, they would almost look like the bones of a cornucopia" . . . and a design detail was born. Who says you can't use multiple pulls on a single door? We installed cylindrical chrome knobs on the sub-top of the cabinet, to support the ½ inch-thick sandblasted glass top. The result is a contemporary cabinet with eye-catching good looks.

GLASS ACT ✛ When I created this custom console for the entry of a client's penthouse, I was inspired to add broken glass in a most unexpected place—on the legs. The glass pieces, which included glass bottles, broken dishes, and bits of sea glass, were selected for their colorful, reflective quality. The glass was embedded in plaster three-quarters of the way down the leg, just above the spade foot. The console itself is made of rosewood with an understated glass top. The pale plaster and brightly colored bits of glass tile really stand out against the dark wood. As an avid art collector, the client was delighted with its one-of-a-kind appeal.

THROUGH THE EYES OF CECIL

A note about transforming a decorative accent item into functional furniture: all furniture has function. But, because furniture must function with body mass and movement, furniture has standard sizes and measurements. Make sure that your designs meet standard furniture measurements.

COMPLETE TRANSFORMATIONS ✤ Simple transformation techniques are fabulous, but what happens when you run into something that needs a complete repurposing? How do you approach this type of transformation? Believe it or not, making a complete transformation doesn't have to be complicated. You just have to be open to possibility.

Transformation is not about using orange crates for storage or the huge phone company cable spools for dining tables. You might have gotten away with it in college, but it's a definite decorative no-no for the over-twenty crowd. At the end of the transformation you want a functional decorative item that may be quirky, but doesn't scream, "We have absolutely no furniture budget!"

Some complete transformations repurpose an object into something it wasn't originally intended to be. Here's an example: Aunt Connie gave you a pair of large ceramic vases, which you planned to use at either end of your fireplace mantle. Unfortunately, you dropped one and shattered it (oops!). Now, you still want to honor Aunt Connie, but it just won't work to display a lone vase on the mantle. Instead, you transform that lone vase completely by turning it into a beautiful decorative lamp.

Of course, a complete transformation is not always so straightforward. Often it's about finding an awesome piece of furniture (an old bar console comes to mind), an interesting object (such as a part of an airplane engine), and/or an unusual find (perhaps a pair of carved legs from a vintage pool table) and totally reworking them as a components in something completely unexpected—like an entertainment cabinet.

THAI TIEBACKS ✤ These leftover pieces of a carved Asian screen were not large, but they were interesting and I couldn't bear to discard them. Ultimately I used them to create tieback details for my conference room window treatment, where they never fail to attract comment. See the buffet unit on page 154 where I used the same screen as door handles

STAND CORRECTED ✛ This is a great story about an Indonesian gong stand I found that I just knew longed to be a coffee table, with the detailed carving as a focal point of the new design. Since coffee tables typically vary from 15 to 24 inches high, before cutting into the gong stand, I had to establish which part of it would serve as the new table's legs. Two of the future coffee table legs were no-brainers because the original pair of carved gong legs was perfect. But, it required a lot more imagination to find the remaining pair. Ultimately, I saw that two legs of the right size, proportion, and design, could be made from the stem of the gong stand. Once the base was made, the 5 foot dragon carving was placed at the top. Other elements of the gong provided structural support as well as pure embellishment.

MOROCCAN STYLE ✛ The fine detail work that is found in some Moroccan screens intrigues me. The craftsmanship (e.g. the smoothness of wood) is not always the best, but the intricacies of the designs are phenomenal. The turnings and shapes commonly found on the screen designs would be very costly to fabricate in the United States. However, they are relatively inexpensive to acquire from Moroccan and Middle Eastern import shops. Just be aware that wooden turnings may be quite rough and require smoothing before you can use the pieces as you envision. (And be aware that sanding the rough parts is a hands-on, time-consuming process.) That being said, these large screens always fire my imagination. As I look at them, I envision using them as part of new and exciting transformations, or repurposing them as completely new things.

Years ago, I purchased a wonderful Moroccan screen from a store whose name I have, unfortunately, long forgotten. The screen was framed out and laid on top of a table base, then topped with glass, as part of a dining table. The intricate carved screen made for a beautiful decorative detail. Sadly, however, I have no photos to share with you.

In keeping with my personal "chicken soup" philosophy, the leftover screen parts from the dining table (about 20 percent of the original screen) were later used to create this 20 inch x 36 inch coffee table for my office. The four balls at the tip end of the legs are new features added to the original parts of the screen. So, don't throw away the parts of an item if they have good bones. In the world of creative detailing, there is nothing better than getting two items for the price of one!

A GREAT PAIR OF LEGS ✤ While shopping at a small collectibles store, I spied two carved wooden animal legs. At 17 inches high, they were the perfect height for something . . . but what? I was so intrigued that I tracked down a salesperson who told me that they had come from an old (Victorian?) billiard table. I was enchanted: Four legs would make a great stand for a coffee table, I thought. My elation rapidly faded, however, when I learned that there were only two legs. I hadn't a clue what I was going to do with two, but I just had to have those legs. So they came home with me. Within weeks I had the vision: I would use them as wall brackets for a console!

JUST PLANE FUN ✤ One of my favorite transformation stories began with the purchase of an airplane engine turbine, which was subsequently turned into a showstopper coffee table in my client's contemporary living room. I can't take credit for the idea, since I bought it in a store for that purpose; but ever since I added the glass tabletop and installed it in my client's home it has been the subject of great conversation. Not a person who enters the house fails to comment on this detail, and visitors are always surprised to learn that it is actually part of an airplane engine! My client and I both love to tell the tale of this transformation.

OPPOSITE ✤ BAR NONE ✤ The moment I saw this traditional bar cabinet, I knew what its new life function would be. The size and shape of the cabinet was perfect for it to be repackaged into a vanity console!

The bar was 3 feet wide, 3 feet high, and 2 feet deep, and in a demilune (or half-round) shape. The transformation required a new top to house the under-mounted sink and faucet. For durability, granite was chosen to replace the original wood. Because it was originally a bar cabinet, the inside of the curved doors were already detailed with holders for wineglasses, I thought it would be best to keep the doors closed for the vanity. Boy, was I wrong!

During the client's decorative (furniture, art, and accessories) installation, the cabinet doors happened to be open on this particular unit, and when I saw the glass holders I thought, "What fabulous towel holders those would make." The look was so divine—various colored hand towels standing at attention in those holders—it demanded that the doors never be closed again!

It may take a lot of brainpower for the average

adult to think creatively, but not the average

child. As children, detailing an existing item

was part of who we were. Adding paint or

crayon to anything reachable, cutting shapes

into anything that could be cut, changing

things because the creative mind directed it—it

is all part of the childhood learning process.

Having creative thoughts is youthful thinking,

so think creatively and stay young.

THROUGH THE
EYES OF CECIL

When creating detail furniture for children (or

adults!) keep in mind that the amount of hard-

ware should not be based on the drawer or

door count. The concept of designing and

detailing cabinet fronts—and possibly sides!—

will be inspired by the artistic details incorpo-

rated in with the theme hardware.

USING DECORATIVE DETAILS TO CREATE THEMES

Why is it that when it comes to children's rooms we do not hesitate to create crafty, artistic concepts? It seems that we want our children to be in environments that encourage both learning and imagination, and we instinctively know that anything goes. But why shouldn't that concept apply to adult theme rooms as well? I say that there's no reason why it can't!

Theme rooms can be simple or complex. They can depend upon furniture items, wall finishes, even decorative hardware, to establish the theme. At one end of the spectrum, they are about taking a central decorative detail (or idea) and building a finished interior around it. At the opposite end, complex theme suites are an amalgamation of all the elements into a one-of-a-kind interior. This is very popular technique for everything from children's bedrooms to honeymoon suites.

In this section we will explore theme concepts focusing on the following means of creating themes for both children and adults:

✣ Furniture pieces
✣ Painted murals and wall scenes
✣ Combination elements (furnishings combined with decorative
   wall treatments)

KID-FRIENDLY THEME SPACES: FURNITURE AND MURALS

In recent years, there has been an explosion of interest in creating themed environments for children. Whether the application is an infant nursery, a toddler bedroom, or a teenager's hideaway, it seems that everyone loves the idea of a fun, funky space for the kids. Depending on the age of the child (not to mention the parents' budget!), kids rooms can be pseudo-realistic or completely fantasy-inspired in design. Some families prefer to splurge on decorative furnishing pieces and keep the remainder of the décor very simplistic. Others rely on painted wall treatments for effect (because parents often choose to purchase pragmatic furnishings that can grow with the child). However, if you choose to combine decorative furnishings with decorative paint treatments, the results can be extraordinary.

FURNITURE DESIGNS TO GROW ON ✣ Detailing furniture for children can be as simple as selecting theme hardware. When it comes to theme hardware, there are literally dozens of types choose from, all of which have been designed specifically to appeal to children. Once you decide on the furniture piece receiving the hardware, the overall design and dimensions of that piece will help you determine the style, design, and amount of hardware you'll need to purchase.

To create these concepts, I enlisted the aid of talented faux finish artist, Wendy Tortollini. She far exceeded my wildest expectations!

It only requires six basketballs to animate the ball in motion from hand to hoop. Again, the artwork completes the basketball theme, which is a favorite of staff members and artist alike. From professional ballplayer to awestruck spectators, this creation is sure to delight.

The player punts . . . will the home team score? Six football knobs take the pigskin through the goal posts for the field goal that wins the game with no time on the clock. The crowd goes wild!

THROUGH THE
EYES OF CECIL

When creating detail furniture for children (or adults!) keep in mind that the amount of hardware should not be based on the drawer or door count. The concept of designing and detailing cabinet fronts—and possibly sides!—will be inspired by the artistic details incorporated in with the theme hardware.

Why not create a flower garden? Fourteen flower pulls—roses and ox-eyed daisies—were used to create the garden. Only six, however, are functional and used to open and close the drawers; the others are purely decorative. Grass, sky, flowers, stems, leaves, even ladybugs and birds, were all hand-painted by the artist.

These three bears have nothing to do with Goldilocks. They're skydiving amidst colorful balloons, and floating down the beautiful blue door front on umbrella-like parachutes. This one is just for fun!

USING PAINT TO CREATE A THEME ✤ Sometimes you may want to establish your theme with faux finishes and decorative painting instead of with specialty furnishings. This is a wonderful way to create design detail on the walls, especially if you want to create the décor in stages.

CREATING THE COMPLETE THEME ROOM:*Combining Customized Furnishings with Painted Murals* ✤ Every child has a dream about who they want to be. While they are in this precious dream stage, create a dream room for them. When I have the rare opportunity to create a child's dream room, I feel like I am going to Disney World! To me, the child's dream room is the Magic Kingdom of theme room designing and gives you the chance to use your imagination and decorative detailing to the max. The fact is parents will have as much fun designing and installing dream room details as a child at Disney World. I've used decorative murals to give flavor to many of my designs for children's rooms. Whether used in combination with ordinary furniture or theme furnishings, the result is always charming.

Because I so rarely get requests to design children's theme rooms, I have turned to master craftsman and internationally renowned furniture designer Mark Wilkinson for some of his beautiful children's rooms. Mark's furniture designs are delightful, and his total theme room installations are breathtaking. I hope you enjoy them as much as I did.

Circus aficionados will appreciate this re-creation of the world of Tom Thumb under the big top. Creative murals turn the room into the inside of a circus tent. Sturdy furnishings recreate the no-frills décor of bleachers and circus props.
Design and photo © Mark Wilkinson Furniture

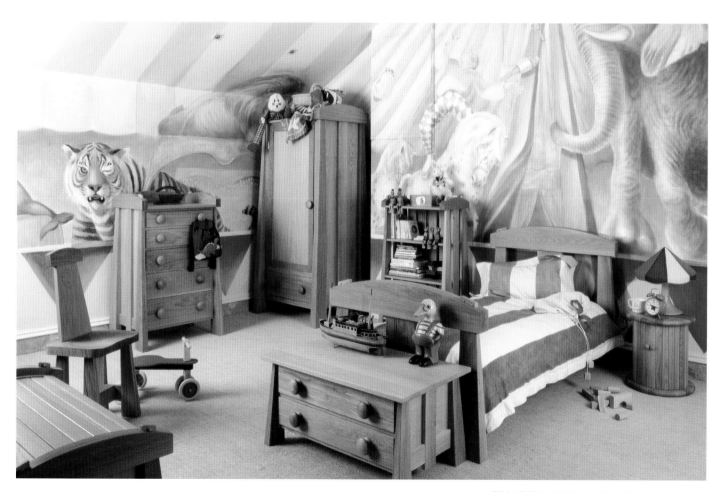

The ultimate princess room combines creative murals with fabulous furnishings. It's just slightly after midnight, judging from the painted clock on the tower of the princess's castle—an imaginative armoire. And everywhere, her Royal Highness's cipher is evident: from the royal dressing table, to the royal chair, right down to the painted crest on the door of her traveling coach. The royal coach itself has been transformed into the most unusual and romantic bed that any little girl could dream of.   Design and photo © Mark Wilkinson Furniture

This room takes its theme from children's fairy tales. (The wall mural depicts the classic tale of *Jack and the Beanstalk*, complete with oversized beanstalk and the giant's castle pictured up in the clouds.) Theme furnishings include an armoire/closet installation shaped like a castle, complete with turrets, guards, and French fleur de lis; a castle-shaped toy chest; and a compatibly designed toddler bed. Design and photo © Mark Wilkinson Furniture

Sometimes it can be difficult to come up with a theme for the young men in our lives. Of course, sports themes are always appropriate, but what to do when the boy in your life isn't a sports fan? One novel approach took its inspiration from King Arthur himself. Using a simple painted mural, the room re-creates the feeling of a timbered medieval dwelling. The furnishings take inspiration from *The Sword in the Stone*, which is about King Arthur and his sword, Excalibur. The sword, shield, and medieval lance can all be found in the furniture details. Carved shields and sword hilts form handles and drawer pulls, while the combination of battle shield and sheathed sword forms the backs of chairs and the mirror detailing. Finally, for the young knight's bed, the designer used lances to detail the headboard, and sheathed swords to detail the footboard. Design and photo © Mark Wilkinson Furniture

GROWN-UP THEME ROOMS: BILLIARDS AND MOVIES

Theme-inspired rooms for adults have always been popular, although they have tended to rely more heavily on furnishings and accessories than on murals and decorative painting techniques. In my design practice these rooms usually take the form of billiard/game rooms and home cinemas.

Adult theme rooms often magnify the decorative inspiration for the home. For example, the overall decorative theme for one home was "fire and ice." We played upon those elements in our design for the homeowner's media room. For another homeowner, we used elements and objects from his profession to define direction for his billiard room décor. I have also created theater and cinema-inspired interiors in my residential design work.

As with any theme-inspired décor, the first step is to determine what you truly need the room to accomplish. Secondly, you need to determine what direction the design is going to take (i.e., what is its inspiration?). One of the benefits of designing the adult theme room is the opportunity to make use of exotic and unusual (read *expensive*) materials.

Less playful, the contemporary billiard room in my client's home is all about being sleek and sophisticated. This design, which pairs a large aquarium and sleek painted glass finish with glass wallpaper and stainless steel accents, is more formal in feel, but no less a reflection of its owner's personality. The room follows the "fire and ice" theme of the home—complete with reflective surfaces. The aquarium was intended to create a focal point in the space.

BILLIARD AND GAME ROOMS ✤ Billiard and game room designs are all about creating funky spaces in which to have fun. Some rooms are more serious than others, but all should reflect the owner's personality. These rooms require careful planning to assure there is adequate space and proper lighting to play all the games. You want to make sure your furniture layout leaves plenty of room to make a shot from all sides and corners of a pool table, for example.

This billiard room was designed for an NFL player, which you may have already figured out. At the time he was playing for the New England Patriots, so it was natural to use their team colors (red, white, and blue) in the décor. All-Star jerseys and helmets signed by friends throughout the NFL reflect his professional identity, just in case he doesn't shoot pool like Minnesota Fats. I even had his name spelled out in the carpeting. Add to all that the central piece of furniture—a custom stainless steel pool table—and scatter in a few bar stools and some small tables and you've got a room that doesn't rely upon painted murals or fantasy furniture, but has definite personality and style. From the floor to the walls, the room design is all about the owner and a just little bit about billiards. Rack 'em up!

HOME THEATERS ✤ What I like about designing home theater installations is that these rooms are all about entertainment. Generally, if there is one room in the house where the homeowner is willing to be creative and playful, this is it. That makes them fun spaces for possible theme decors.

All home theaters must offer the following: a place for the video and audio equipment, comfortable seating, the ability to black out the room for comfortable viewing, and some sort of soundproofing system. One of the first steps in my home cinema designs is to cover the wall(s) with upholstered panels. Not only do they provide a central design detail in the room (I like to use them as primary elements in creating a theme décor), they also perform the purely functional role of deadening sound.

This room is designed around a movie theater theme, complete with concession stands. Accessed through an archway from the adjoining game room, the theme begins with the entrance, which is topped by a marquee proclaiming the cinema's name. The red, white, and blue color scheme carries through from the game room into the cinema and concession stand area. A series of stainless steel columns accents the upholstered red walls of the room. A raised platform creates stadium-style seating to afford optimal viewing. Reclining theater seats line the rear wall, while a custom-built lounger for two occupies the center of the room. The audio/visual equipment, which is not shown, adorns the wall immediately facing the loungers. The whole project was created in what was intended to be a slightly larger than usual guest room.

Custom upholstered walls marry a series of undulating shapes into a cohesive whole in this large residential theater. Three layers of stadium-style seating ensure optimal viewing. Each layer is outfitted with an upholstered recliner in royal blue and cushioned seating in gray. The foremost layer features a full-sized reclining lounger. Granite-topped V-ball side tables also provide storage. Lighting comes from a series of lighted glass columns with stainless steel collars.

The cinema screen is flanked by a pair of stainless steel torches. The columns are actually topped with stained glass "flames" and lit from within by flickering lightbulbs. Overhead, the coffered ceiling is outfitted with fiber-optics lighting to create the illusion of a night sky full of twinkling stars.

LET'S REVIEW

Decorative detailing is almost always the result of a spark to the imagination. You can take this creative inspiration and put it to use in many ways, but two of my favorite involve transforming found objects and creating theme environments.

There is no law that says a "found" object cannot be repurposed. The exciting challenge, of course, is to find that new purpose or decorative use for the items that catch your eye. When you spot that special something, you should not be afraid to purchase it, even if you're not quite certain how you will use it. The new purpose isn't always immediately apparent, but if you hang on to it and think about it once a week or so, you will eventually be inspired with its creative purpose.

Repurposed items can be either completely transformed, such as the gong stand that became my coffee table, or used as a decorative additive, like the set of Ethiopian horn spoons that became cabinet pulls for my buffet.

The other type of decorative detailing is probably the one that appeals to most people—creating decorative themes. Theme rooms can be created for both adult and children's rooms, although I think most people are more comfortable with children's rooms, probably because they make us feel free to let the rules fly out the window. As long as the room is safe for our children and encourages both learning and imagination, we don't seem to get as uptight about doing it "right" as we do for the adult rooms in our homes.

Theme rooms can be created using decorative furnishings, decorative painting, or a combination of the two, and can be as playful or as sophisticated as desired. If decorative furnishings will form the focus of the theme design, don't forget the small details. Even decorative doorknobs and hardware can add immeasurably to a theme. Decorative painting, in the form of murals and painted furnishings, can be as lifelike or as fantastic as desired. I am particularly fond of tromp l'oeil (fool the eye) treatments, which combine paint with three-dimensional accents. When all elements—furnishings, painting, and three-dimensional accents—are combined, paint has the advantage of bringing the whole creation to life. The detail items and furnishings can then be used to reinforce and continuously re-create the theme.

THROUGH THE EYES OF CECIL

There is a large part of us that wants to be creative. It is part of our nature. During the growing-up process, we have been told to grow up, get serious, rein in the way we do things. In essence, this controlled behavior robbed us of our imagination. So here is your mission today: Throw away the grown-up stuff and have fun detailing a room that no one can say is tacky or overdone. After all, it's not real; it's a dream room!

WORKING DRAWINGS FOR CECIL'S
ORIGINAL FURNITURE DESIGNS

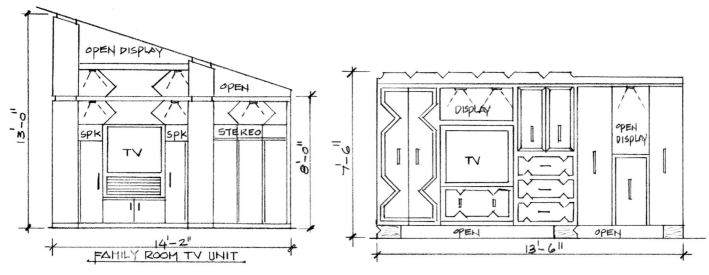

OPEN DISPLAY

OPEN

SPK   SPK   STEREO

13'-0"   TV   8'-0"

14'-2"
FAMILY ROOM TV UNIT

Working drawing for the entertainment unit on page 110

DISPLAY

OPEN DISPLAY

TV

OPEN   OPEN

7'-6"

13'-6"

Working Drawing for the TV/storage unit on page 123

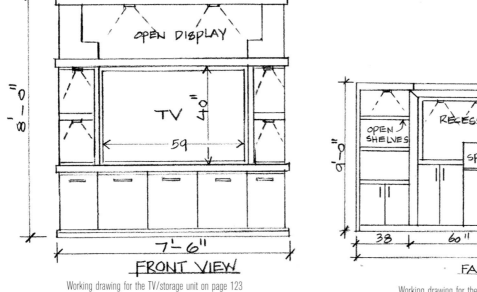

OPEN DISPLAY

TV   4'-0"

59

8'-0"

7'-6"
FRONT VIEW

Working drawing for the TV/storage unit on page 123

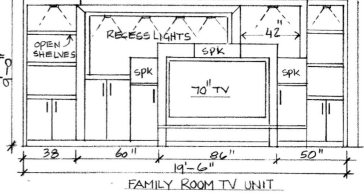

OPEN SHELVES   RECESS LIGHTS   42"

SPK   SPK   SPK

70" TV

8'-0"

38   60"   86"   50"

19'-6"
FAMILY ROOM TV UNIT

Working drawing for the family room entertainment unit on page 124

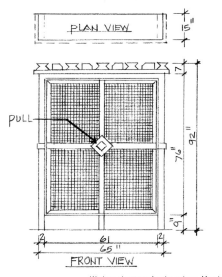

Working drawings for the cabana Murphy bed on page 133

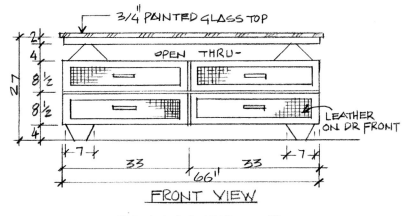

Working drawing for the night table on page 135

All photographs © 2007 Tim Ribar, except as noted below.

DAN FORER is an internationally renowned photographer specializing in architecture and interiors. His work—which has included the homes of Sophia Loren, Cher, Claudette Colbert, Wesley Snipes, Sylvester Stallone, and entrepreneur Richard Branson, among others—has appeared in major design publications such as *Interior Design*, *Architectural Record* and *Architectural Digest*.

ROY QUESADA is a photographer based in South Florida, specializing in advertising and architectural and fine art photography.

TIM RIBAR is a commercial and editorial photographer based in Fort Lauderdale, Florida. His photo career began in high school when he contributed pictures for his sportswriter father's articles in a suburban Philadelphia daily paper. His clients range from *USA Today* and *Guest Informant* hotel books to advertising agencies and colleges and universities. Publication credits include: *Time* magazine, *Golf Digest*, *The New York Times*, *Travel Holiday*, *Florida Design*, *Miami Home & Decor*, and numerous airline in-flight magazines.

Over his three-decade career, KIM SARGENT has established a reputation as one of the country's foremost architectural photographers. His images have been featured in such notable publications as *Architectural Digest*, *Art & Antiques*, *Interior Design*, *Florida Design*, *Metropolitan Home*, *Florida Architecture*, *Veranda*, and *The New York Times Magazine*.

RESOURCES

Here is a list of retailers and resources that may be helpful to you as you design your home. Of course, I strongly suggest that you also take the time to get to know what is available in your community. Not only does it have the advantage of being local, it also gives you the opportunity to see the product for yourself before your buy.

Cecil Hayes (What kind of designer would I be if I didn't recommend myself!)
6601 Lyons Road, #C4
Coconut Creek, FL 33334
(954) 570-5843 or visit www.cecilhayes.com

OPEN TO THE PUBLIC

DEPARTMENT STORES

Macy's (the world's largest department store)
Visit a store near you or shop online at
www.macys.com

Stein Mart (upscale, off-price specialty store chain)
www.steinmart.com

Target (affordable interior décor available nationwide)
Visit a store near you or shop online at
www.target.com

DESIGN CENTERS

Expo Design Center
Locations in Arizona, California, Florida, Georgia, Illinois, Massachusetts, Maryland, Missouri, New Jersey, New York, Tennessee, Texas, and Virginia.
Visit www.expo.com

Robb & Stucky Inc.
Locations in Arizona, Florida, and Texas.
Visit www.robbstucky.com

FABRICS & TRIMS

Boca Bargoons (Decorative fabric outlet)
Locations in Arizona, California, Colorado, Florida, Georgia, and Texas.
190 N.W. 20 Street
Boca Raton, FL 33431
(561) 392-5700 or visit www.bocabargoons.com

Calico Corners (fabric, furniture and home décor)
800) 213-6366 or visit www.calicocorners.com

Decorator Fabrics, Inc. (A huge selection of upholstery weight fabric & trims)
1249 Sterling Road
Dania, FL 33044
954-925-8685 or visit www.decofab.com

Hancock Fabrics (Decorator fabrics and trims including Waverly)
Has a limited selection of upholstery weight fabrics in stock.
Can also special order selected fabrics.
Visit www.hancockfabrics.com

JoAnn's Fabrics & Crafts (Decorator fabrics and trims including Waverly)Has a limited selection of upholstery weight fabrics in stock.
Can also special order selected fabrics.
Visit www.joann.com

M&J Trimming (Fashion trimmings nirvana!)
Just about any kind of trimming you can think of from nailheads to fur and feathers to ribbon and beads.
Visit www.mjtrim.com

Rag Shop (Very limited selection of decorator fabrics)
Stores in Connecticut, Florida, New Jersey, New York, Pennsylvania
www.ragshop.com

Vintage Fabrics & Etc. (vintage textiles and indigos)
3500 NE 11th Avenue, Suite C
Fort Lauderdale, FL 33334
(954) 564-4392

FURNISHINGS & HOME DECOR

Ballard Designs (traditional furnishings and home décor catalog)
(800) 536-7391 or visit www.ballarddesigns.com

Calico Corners (fabric, furniture and home décor)
(800) 213-6366 or visit www.calicocorners.com

Crate & Barrel (transitional furnishings and home décor)
(800) 967-6696 or visit www.crateandbarrel.com

Design Within Reach (contemporary designer furniture and accessories)
Design studios in 21 states nationwide.
(800) 944-2233 or visit www.dwr.com

Ethan Allen(traditional/transitional furniture and accessories)
Over 300 stores
Visit www.ethanallen.com

Floridian Furniture (urban/contemporary furniture)
4797 SW 8th Street
Miami, FL 33134
(305) 448-2639

High Brow Furniture (modern furniture catalog)
2110 8th Avenue South
Nashville, TN
(888) 329-0219 or visit
www.highbrowfurniture.com

Lands End Home (the popular retailer now has a home division)
1-800-963-4816 or visit www.landsend.com

La-Z-Boy (recliners are back—and they are spectacular!)
Available at retail locations nationwide or visit
www.lazboy.com

Mark Wilkinson Furniture, Inc. (Fabulous handmade furnishings and cabinetry)
Headquarters and Showroom:
Overton House . High Street . Bromham
Nr. Chippenham, Wiltshire SN15 2HA
+44 (0) 1380 850004
www.mwf.com

Mikala, Inc.
6601 Lyons Road
Coconut Creek, FL 33073
(954) 570-5843 or visit www.cecilhayes.com or www.mikalainc.com

Pier 1 Imports (transitional furnishings and home décor)
(800) 245-4595 or visit www.pier1.com

Pottery Barn (transitional furnishings and home décor)
(888) 779-5176 or visit www.potterybarn.com

Restoration Hardware (traditional/retro hardware, furnishings, and home décor)
104 Challenger Drive
Portland, TN 37148-1704
(800) 762-1005 or visit
www.restorationhardware.com

Room and Company (modern furnishings catalog)
(888) 404-7666 or visit
www.roomandcompany.com

Thomasville
Available worldwide
(800) 225-0265 or visit www.thomasville.com

West Elm (urban/modern furnishings)
Stores in California, Georgia, Illinois, New Jersey, New York, Oregon, Texas, Virginia
(866) 937-8356 or visit www.westelm.com

Williams-Sonoma Home (traditional furnishings and home décor)
(877) 812-6235 or visit www.williamssonoma.com

HARDWARE/HOME IMPROVEMENT

Home Depot (home improvement)
Visit www.homedepot.com

Lowe's Home Improvement Warehouse (home improvement)
Visit www.lowes.com

Restoration Hardware (traditional/retro hardware, furnishings, and home décor)
104 Challenger Drive
Portland, TN 37148-1704
(800) 762-1005 or visit
www.restorationhardware.com

LIGHTING

Nightshades (exquisite custom created lampshades by Christine Kilger)
561-750-5181 or visit www.nighshades.com

Shades of Light (lighting, draperies, and more)
4924 W. Broad Street
Richmond, VA
800-262-6612 or visit www.shadesoflight.com

Y-Lighting (contemporary lighting catalog)
(866) 428-9289 or visit www.y-lighting.com

"Special thanks to Stein Mart for helping me reach so many people through my accessories seminars that raise money for Stein Mart's "Dignity U Wear"charity, which provides clothing for children in need."

METAL TILE

Lowitz & Company (hand-cast metal tile)
Makers of Talisman/Foundry Art/Bronzework
Studio
(773) 784-2628 or visit
www.lowitzandcompany.com

MISCELLANEOUS

Get It Right! Furniture Patterns (life-size furniture
templates to make arranging easier)
6601 Lyons Road, #C4
Coconut Creek, FL 33073
(954) 570-5843 or visit www.cecilhayes.com

MOLDING AND PICTURE
FRAME MOLDING

Arquati (picture frame molding)
(800) 527-0421 or visit www.arquatiusa.com

Enkeboll Designs (architectural woodcarvings and
picture frame molding)
(310) 532-1400 or visit www.enkeboll.com

PAINT AND WALLCOVERING

Sherwin Williams (paint and wallpaper)
Visit www.sherwin-williams.com

American Blind and Wallpaper Company (the
name says it all!)
Visit www.decoratetoday.com

WINDOW TREATMENTS

American Blind and Wallpaper company (the
name says it all!)
Visit www.decoratetoday.com

Hunter Douglas (blinds and window treatments)
Visit www.hunterdouglas.com

Shades of Light (lighting, draperies, and more)
4924 W. Broad Street
Richmond, VA
800-262-6612 or visit www.shadesoflight.com

TO THE TRADE

Some home décor items are only available to the
trade, that is, to interior design professionals including architects, interior designers, contractors, and
manufacturers only. These products may be available
directly from the manufacturer, or in retail stores
and design centers. If you are interested in any of
the companies listed below, please call them directly
to find out where you can get their products.

FABRIC

Kravet (fabrics and trims)
225 Central Avenue South
Bethpage, NY 11714
(516) 293-2000 or visit www.kravet.com

Waverly (fabric, wallpaper, and home décor)
Visit www.waverly.com.

LEATHER

Edelman Leather
Teddy & Arthur Edelman Limited
80 Pickett District Road
New Milford, CT 06776
(800) 886-TEDY or visit
www.edelmanleather.com

TILE

Ann Sachs (tiles—stone, glass, ceramic)
(800) 278-8453 or visit www.annsacks.com

Walker-Zanger (tiles—stone, glass, ceramic)
(877) 611-0199 or visit www.walkerzanger.com

WINDOW TREATMENTS

Hart-Lines by Valerie (custom drapery workshop)
1059 SW 30th Avenue
Deerfield Beach, FL 33442
(954) 421-5252

Ravan, Incorporated (custom drapery workshop)
Atlanta, GA and Dania, FL locations
Visit www.ravan-inc.com

TO THE TRADE
DESIGN CENTERS

Note: Each design center has its own policies and
procedures regarding public access and purchases.
It is suggested that you contact your nearest design
center directly for information.

California

Laguna Design Center
23811 Aliso Creek Road
Laguna Niguel, CA 92677

Pacific Design Center
3687 Melrose Avenue
Los Angeles, CA 90069

San Francisco Design Center
2 Henry Adams Street
San Francisco, CA 94103

Florida

Design Center of the Americas (DCOTA)
1855 Griffin Road
Dania Beach, FL 33004

Georgia

Atlanta Decorative Arts Center
351 Peachtree Hills Avenue, NE
Atlanta, GA 30305-4502

Illinois

The Merchandise Mart
Chicago, IL 60654
(800) 677-6278

Massachusetts

Boston Design Center
One Design Center Place
Boston, MA 02210

Michigan

Michigan Design Center
1700 Stutz Drive
Troy, MI 48084

Minnesota

International Market Square
275 Market Street
Minneapolis, MN 55405

New York

New York Design Center
200 Lexington Avenue
New York, NY 10016

Ohio

Ohio Design Centre
23533 Mercantile Road
Beachwood, OH 44122

Pennsylvania

Marketplace Design Center
2400 Market Street
Philadelphia, Pa 19103

Texas

Dallas Design Center
1250 Slocum
Dallas, TX 75207

Decorative Center of Houston
5120 Woodway Drive
Houston, TX 77056

Washington

Seattle Design Center
5701 Sixth Avenue South
Seattle, WA 98108

Washington, DC

Washington Design Center
300 D Street, S.W.
Washington, D.C. 20024

INDEX

A

Absolute Black granite, 32
accent
    motifs, 27
    piece/furniture, 8–9
    wall of color, 10
    accessories
    lampshades, 147–148
    picture frames, 148
architectural details, 24–25,
  90–115
areas that could benefit from
  decorative detailing, 23
art niches. *see* structural art niches

B

backsplash, 18, 56, 59, 60
beach paneling/trim, 23
bedding, 138–140
Black Galaxy granite, 32, 36–37
blinds, 80–81
buffet unit, 4–5, 126, 154

C

canopy beds, 140–141
carpet(s)/rug(s), 28–29
changes in elevation, playing up,
  98–99
colored grout, 37
color(s)
    as design element, 19
    contrasting, 6–7, 35, 36–37,
      110–111, 113
columns, 93–96, 110, 114, 122, 169,
  170
combining multiple flooring
  materials, 35
complete transformations, 156–159
corbel, 6–7
cornices, 85–86
creating a themed environment,
  160–171
    billiards and movies, 168–170
    for adults, 167–170
    for kids, 160–166
creative, definition of, 22
Crema Marfil marble, 32
custom forged ironwork, 154

D

decorative
    definition of, 22
    fabric trims, 76–78, 138, 139,
      140
decorative detailing
    primer, 14–25
    rules, 22
de-emphasizing existing doors,
  70–72
design elements, 17–19
detail, definition of, 22
details can save the day, 54–55
door
    casings, 105
    fronts, 21, 116–117, 152
    knobs vs. touch latch, 73
    pulls, 152, 153, 154, 155, 161,
      166

drapery/draperies, 76–77, 125, 141,
  142
drawer fronts. *see* door fronts
drawer pulls. *see* door pulls

E

elements of design. *see* design
  elements
elevation changes, 98–99

F

fabric and soft covering details, 8–9,
  14, 19–20, 68–69, 136–149
    bedding, 138–140
    skirted tables, 144
    slipcovers, 144
    throw pillows, 145–147
    trims, 76–78, 138, 139
    versatility of, 137
faux finishes/paint, 48–49, 50–51,
  52–53, 90–91, 116–117, 163
fireplaces, 100–102
flooring details, 26–37
furniture details, 21, 116–135
    bar cabinet, 158–159
    bathroom vanities, 128,
    buffets, 4–5, 126, 154
    closet storage, 130–131
    coffee table, 157, 158
    desks, 127
    entertainment and wall units,
      118–125
    Murphy beds, 132–133
    night tables, 127, 134
    powder baths, 129

G

glass, 30, 35, 37, 38–39, 52–53, 56,
  59, 65, 96–97, 100, 103, 114,
  116–117, 155, 167, 170
granite, 35, 36–37, 116–117, 153,
  170

H

hemline(s)/hem(s)
    bedding, 139
    drapery, 77

I

installations
    nonstructural, 107–109, 115
    structural, 92–106, 115

K

karate-chop, decorator-style, 145, 146
Kilger, Christine, 147

L

lampshades, 147–148
large-scale decorative detailing, 21
leather
    detailing, on floors, 30–31
    faux, 46–47
    upholstery, on furniture, 134
limestone, 26–27, 61
linings, 77

M

marble, 24, 26–27, 32–33, 35, 62–63,
  100
metal
    and doors, 105
    and flooring, 30, 35

and furniture, 126
and walls, 50–51
Mikala Collection, 116
Mirroflex, 56–57
mirror, 52–53, 94–95, 166
molding(s), 14, 40, 69, 139
    baseboard, 44, 47, 51
    -based window treatments, 84
    carved, 6–7, 73
    chair rail, 44
    crown, 41–42, 47, 115
    custom, 43
    dental, 47, 87
    flat, 123
    for interior and exterior doors,
      103–106
    frame, 44
    Japanese ash, 50–51, 83
    picture, 21, 153, 73
    profile, 123
    replaces artwork, 45
    and shoji screens, 83
    silver leaf, 46–47, 52, 128
    stone tile, 44
    used on furniture, 4–5, 152
    used to create pelmets, 87
    vertical, 46–47
    and wallpaper, 44
mosaic, 26–27, 58–59
murals, 163, 165

N

nonstructural installations, 107–109,
  115

O

ornate, definition of, 22
overview of text, 12–13

P

paint, 48–49, 56, 73
paneling, wood, 63–64, 66–67,
  104–105, 114
pelmet(s) 87, 154
picture frames, 148
pillow. *see* fabric and soft covering
  details
pillow fills, 145
plastic laminate(s), 56, 153
pleats, 76
polyurethane, 8–9, 34
puck light/spotlight, 112, 115

R

Rudy Art Glass Studio, 52
rug(s). *see* carpet(s)/rug(s)
rules for decorative detailing, 22

S

Saturnia marble, 32–33
screen(s), 74–75, 82–83, 89,
  150–151, 154, 156, 157
shade(s), 81
shape, as design element, 17–18
shoji screens, 74–75, 82–83, 89
simple transformations, 152–155
skirted tables, 144
slipcovers, 144
soffit(s), 90–91, 92, 94–95, 101, 107,
  114
soft details. *see* fabric and soft cover
  ing details
split travertine, 24–25

spotlight. *see* puck light/spotlight
stainless steel, 38–39, 50–51, 69,
  96–97, 100, 101, 128, 167, 168,
  169, 170
staircases and steps, 96–97
stair riser, 98–99
stone, 32–33, 35, 37, 59, 61–63,
  94–95, 100, 101
structural art niches, 111–113, 115
structural installations, 92–106, 115
    columns, 93–96
    fireplaces, 100–102
    soffits, 90–91, 92, 94–95, 101
    staircases and steps, 96–97

T

texture, as design element, 18
throw pillows, 145–147
tiebacks, 78, 79 156
tile, 26–27, 35, 73, 102, 107, 139
    ceramic, 17–19, 28, 35, 37,
      58–61
    inset, 36–37, 107
    "rug", 32
tin-type appeal, 51
Tortollini, Wendy, 161
transformation imagination, 150–171
    creating a themed environ
      ment, 160–171
    definition of, 151
    reworking a found item,
      151–159
transforming boxy spaces, 114–115
transforming/reworking a found
  item, 151–159
trims, 76–78, 138, 139, 140
turn-back, 138–139
TVs, plasma, 57

U

unusual art pieces, 14
upholstered
    armchairs, 142
    dining chairs, 142
    headboards, 140
    stools, 8–9
    walls, 136–137, 169, 170

V

valance(s), 77–78, 80–81

W

wall and trim details, 6–7, 38–73
wallpaper, 44, 47, 48, 54, 73
wainscot detailing, 44
welting, 142
Wilkinson, Mark, 163–166
window details/options, 6–7, 74–89
    combination treatments, 86–88
    hard treatments, 82–85, 88
    ready-made treatments, 88, 89
    soft treatments, 76–81, 89
wood, 34, 35, 37, 61, 63–67, 82–85,
  88, 105, 124, 125, 126, 127, 128,
  129, 130, 139
wood paneling. *see* paneling, wood
wrought-iron ornamentation, 154

Z

zebrawood, 110, 172